A Geographia Guide

East Anglia

Norfolk, Suffolk, Cambridge,
Ely and North Essex

INCLUDING

  HUNSTANTON
  GREAT YARMOUTH
  THE BROADS
  NORWICH
  LOWESTOFT
  SOUTHWOLD
  FELIXSTOWE
  IPSWICH
  BURY ST. EDMUNDS
  CLACTON-ON-SEA
  CONSTABLE COUNTRY
  COLCHESTER
  CAMBRIDGE
  NEWMARKET
  ELY

 **Geographia Ltd**
63 Fleet Street
London, EC4Y 1PE

Guide to East Anglia
ISBN 0 09 205520 6
© Geographia Ltd.,
63 Fleet Street,
London, EC4Y 1PE

Compiled and published by
Geographia Ltd

Contributors:
H. O. Wade, text
W. Balmain, line illustrations
 and 'Wildlife'
P. G. Robson, B.Sc., 'Geology'

Maps by Geographia Ltd

Photographic illustrations
by courtesy of
The British Tourist Authority
with the exception of
Lowestoft—Ford Jenkins
Earsham—The Otter Sanctuary—Philip Wayre

Series Editor: J. T. Wright

Made and printed in
Great Britain by
The Anchor Press Ltd,
Tiptree, Essex

Contents

	Page
Section 1 Introduction	5
The National Trust	8
Getting About—Walking, Cycling, Camping and Caravanning, Motoring	9
Wildlife	10
Geology	13
English Tourist Board	18
Section 2 Norfolk Coast	19
King's Lynn, Hunstanton, Sheringham, Cromer, Great Yarmouth	
Section 3 The Broads	38
Section 4 The Norwich Area	41
Norwich; Norwich to North Walsham, Blickling Hall, and Aylsham; Norwich to Walsingham, Fakenham, and East Dereham; Norwich to Wymondham, Diss, and Bungay	
Section 5 Breckland	63
Swaffham, Downham Market, Thetford	
Section 6 East Suffolk Coast	67
Lowestoft, Southwold, Aldeburgh, Felixstowe	
Section 7 Inland Suffolk	76
Ipswich, Woodbridge, Sutton Hoo, Beccles, Bury St. Edmunds, Stowmarket, Needham Market	
Section 8 North Essex Coast	91
Harwich and Dovercourt, Walton-on-the-Naze, Clacton-on-Sea, Holland-on-Sea, Jaywick Sands, Brightlingsea, West Mersea, Maldon	
Section 9 The Constable Country, etc.,	99
Sudbury, Hadleigh, Dedham Vale, Cavendish, Long Melford, Lavenham, Finchingfield, Braintree, Colchester	
Section 10 Cambridge and the Isle of Ely	112
Cambridge, Newmarket, Ely, March, Wisbech	
Alphabetical Index	125

Illustrations

Photographs:

	Facing Page		Facing Page
Bury St. Edmunds	96	East Bergholt	81
Cambridge	97	Ely	97
Castle-Acre	49	Holkham	33
Cavendish	81	King's Lynn	32
Coggeshall	96	Lowestoft	80
Earsham	49	Norwich	48

Drawings:

	Page		Page
The Avocet	11	Maldon	98
Blickling Hall	47	Nayland	101
Cambridge	116	Norfolk Wherry	38
Colchester	111	Ricklinghall Inferior	79
Diss	62	St. Osyth	95
East Dereham	55	Thetford	66
Framlingham Castle	82	Wicken Fen	124
Ipswich	90		

Maps

	Page		Page
Cambridge	114	Ipswich	77
Clacton-on-Sea	93	King's Lynn	20
Colchester	107	Norwich	45
Great Yarmouth	34	The Broads	128

Every reasonable care has been taken to ensure that the information in this Guide is correct at the time of going to press. Nevertheless, the Publishers can accept no responsibility for errors or omissions or for changes in the details quoted.

Section 1 Introduction

THE NAME 'EAST ANGLIA' REFERS to a piece of country that has no exact boundaries and no political or local government connotations. Yet it is a complete and easily recognisable area that was a kingdom in Saxon days. The derivation of the name was from the district of the 'East Angles', which was divided in its turn into 'North Folk' and 'South Folk', or, as we say, Norfolk and Suffolk. The adjoining kingdom was that of the 'East Saxons' (Essex in modern parlance), which in those days included the land belonging to the 'Middle Angles' and stretched as far as what we know as Cambridge and the Isle of Ely. Thus, by long historic and poetic association, these areas are popularly thought of as comprising 'East Anglia', though very strictly it is bounded by Norfolk and Suffolk. However, it is clear from the ample precedence provided by such established works as *Green's History of the English People*, and from maps delineating the divisions of Saxon England, that 'poetic licence' in the matter is not out of place.

Peaceful Charm

Today the area retains the characteristics that made it a complete unit, somewhat different from anywhere else, with its roots in the past. This past is more apparent than in many other localities in these islands. The chief reason for this delightful state of affairs is simply that the Industrial Revolution of the seventeenth, eighteenth and nineteenth centuries virtually passed by East Anglia, leaving little after-effect and no scars. In East Anglia there is no coal and there are no fast-flowing rivers from which to obtain power, the first requirement of the early industrialists. Consequently East Anglia has preserved many of the charms that have been destroyed in other parts of Britain since the years of industrialisation.

Bracing Climate

Physically, East Anglia is flat, few parts rising more than 300 feet above sea-level. The rainfall is low and the climate generally bracing, though subject in early spring to east winds and the occasional onslaught of 'sea fret', that light sea mist which frequently besets the sea coast and, sometimes, invades the land many miles from the sea. However, these slight disadvantages serve only to highlight the exceptionally sunny weather throughout the summer months.

East Anglia may be divided into sections each of which has its own distinct features, to some extent its own way of life and certainly its own history.

EAST ANGLIA

THE COAST

SINCE HISTORY WAS FIRST RECORDED this coast has been subject to flooding and erosion to a greater extent than any other comparable length of coastline in Britain, so that, to a greater or lesser degree, in certain parts this has entailed a continual fight against the sea. Whilst on most coasts this age-old battle concerns only the fishermen and seamen, in the Fens, the marshes and river deltas, and areas of agricultural land subject to flooding, it involves a large proportion of the inland population also.

The coastal inhabitants are mainly seamen, and are noted for their toughness and endurance. In the marshy areas around the Wash, or among the river deltas, the people became wildfowlers, reed-gatherers, or inshore fisherman, following, in short, the diverse occupations natural to such areas. Thus the coastal population of East Anglia has contributed much to Britain's sea power and many Norfolk and Suffolk men were among the earliest colonists in the eighteenth and nineteenth centuries.

Now, in spite of the decline of our fishing fleets, Lowestoft remains one of the great fishing ports.

THE BROADS

THE BROADS ARE A VERY SPECIAL AREA INDEED, and not duplicated anywhere else in these islands. From Horsey Mere in the north, to the River Waveney in the south, a distance of some twenty miles, it is almost as though the opposing gods of the land and the water had reached a compromise over the area each should occupy, and, after aeons of competition, peace had settled over this countryside. For the fisherman, the wildfowler and those who like 'messing about in boats', this is a paradise. The motorist in this region may be surprised when he finds that he may motor all day and never see the Broads themselves; he will see, sometimes, a sail or the upper parts of a motor-launch behind a bank, but seldom the water itself, unless he drives to one of the many little harbours or tie-ups. Perhaps because of this element of surprise Broadland is not only extremely beautiful but in many ways unique.

AGRICULTURAL NORFOLK

NORFOLK (APART FROM THE BROADS, BRECKLAND and the Fens) is almost entirely agricultural in character and occupation. This has been so since man first cultivated these rich lands. Today, Norfolk may appear, at the first superficial exploration, to be one huge arable farm with little stock and somewhat lacking in the natural beauties to be found farther south. Nothing could be further from the truth; hidden away there are farms where the traditional livestock policy is still practised and, if the motorist leaves the main roads and seeks out the by-ways and little-known villages, he will find an abundance of natural beauty and, in particular, some very lovely churches. East Anglia is rightly famed for the magnificence of its village churches, built largely in the fifteenth, sixteenth and seventeenth centuries. This was the long period of the dominance of sheep-farming, and the prosperity of the sheep-farmers in the centuries of heavy demand for wool led to richly endowed churches—hence 'Wool Churches'.

BRECKLAND

BRECKLAND STRETCHES IN A NARROW BAND running from north to south between the rich agricultural lands of Norfolk and Suffolk and the fens of Cambridgeshire. Heath, forest and flint are the chief features of the region. It is very little changed over the centuries, apart from the plantings of the Forestry Commission. Sparsely populated, this is a land for the walker and the family intent upon enjoying the open air with room to breathe and play. Here there are a number of ancient trackways beckoning the walker and, since hills are almost non-existent, the going is extremely easy.

SUFFOLK

SUFFOLK, SOMEWHAT SOFTER AND SLIGHTLY HILLIER in aspect than her northern neighbour, has more apparent natural beauties. Here the agricultural student will see more livestock, although the modern tendency is towards arable cropping. One of the most outstanding features of the small towns and villages of Suffolk is the large number of genuine half-timbered houses, cottages and inns of the Tudor period. Some of these villages have remained almost unchanged over hundreds of years, some have been extended delightfully and with excellent taste, while others have been ruined by modern building totally out of harmony with the original appearance of the places. The village churches of Suffolk are, if possible, even finer and larger than those of Norfolk.

CONSTABLE COUNTRY

THE ENCHANTING 'CONSTABLE COUNTRY' is named after one of Britain's greatest landscape painters. It is a quite small area, along both sides of the River Stour, thus it includes southern Suffolk and the northern parts of Essex. This is a land of unbelievable beauties, of streams and woods, of hills and tiny valleys, of villages and hamlets that have remained almost unchanged over the centuries. One or two spots have been commercialised but, on the whole, this small section of country remains as Constable knew it.

THE FENS

THE FENS INCLUDE MOST OF CAMBRIDGESHIRE. This is a land of black soil and waterways, of far vistas dotted with red-roofed farmhouses, of small farms with a tremendous potential, of little villages reflecting only the changing seasons and the seasons' work. This is not really holiday-maker's-land at all, yet it has an attraction that is difficult to define, as well as a history full of interest, being an epic account of man's long struggle with, and partial victory over, the forces of nature.

THE NATIONAL TRUST

THIS NOW WIDELY ACCLAIMED ORGANISATION was founded in 1895, the brain-child of Miss Octavia Hill, Canon H. D. Rawnsley and Sir Robert Hunter. Their idea was to call a halt to the destruction of the English countryside, towns and villages, by the remorseless march of industrialisation.

They decided to call their new movement 'The National Trust', and from the first it has remained unsponsored by Government, and has relied upon membership subscriptions, charitable donations and bequests.

A body of responsible people was formed to administer its funds, as trustees, acting for the people of the nation, buying lovely areas of countryside so that they might be nature reserves, as well as places of recreation, acquiring properties of archaeological interest, fine old houses, places with historic, literary and artistic associations, or any others which were threatened with destruction.

One of the glories of the work of The National Trust is the sensitive manner in which the properties have been maintained. Some house unique collections of silver, china, or antique furniture: others have art galleries on the premises, and there are those like Blickling Hall in Norfolk where there is not only a formal garden, but also a park designed after the style of Capability Brown.

The Parliament Act of 1907 conferred upon The National Trust the unique right to declare its lands, and most of its properties, inalienable —meaning that they can never be mortgaged or sold, nor compulsorily acquired without the special permission of Parliament.

The general public has, as a rule, free access to the land owned by the Trust, and at properties where an admission fee is charged, there is a privilege free admission to Members of the Trust upon production of their membership cards.

Today the whole nation is vastly indebted to The National Trust for the preservation of whole stretches of glorious coastline which otherwise could have been despoiled, as well as all the other areas of great beauty or special interest.

GETTING ABOUT

THE WALKER WHO WISHES TO SEE and explore some part of East Anglia can make a very pleasant holiday on foot in this beautiful countryside. The coast offers an attractive but not strenuous two weeks' walk. Over the southern portion, marshes and mud-flats obstruct progress and necessitate many detours. For the naturalist this is perhaps the ideal walk. For the walker who likes to cover ten to fifteen miles per day then Great Yarmouth should be the starting-point. From here, north-westwards to Hunstanton is almost all hard and unobstructed walking.

Inland the heaths of Breckland offer some fine, if level, terrain. Holme-next-the-Sea, near Hunstanton, and the nearby village of Ringstead are at the northern end of Peddar's Way: this is an ancient trackway that has never been fully explained, but can be followed for twelve or fifteen miles southwards. Between Swaffham and Downham Market, or Swaffham, Thetford and Bury St. Edmunds, there is some fine open heathland interspersed with forest.

The rest of East Anglia is agricultural country over which, in many places, footpaths are fairly plentiful. For the walker who likes a green and pleasant land this should make a good stamping ground, with accommodation every few miles.

The Fens can offer little attraction to the walker, unless he is a student whose studies take him to the black soil and the waterways.

Cycling

There are few hills in East Anglia to trouble the cyclist, and the area has so much beauty and charm hidden from the main roads that a cycle is possibly the ideal form of transport. C.T.C. members can always obtain help and advice from their Club.

Camping and Caravanning

A camping holiday can be great fun. It is often an excellent solution for families with lively, active children who find the atmosphere of hotels restrictive, and it is comparatively inexpensive. If you wish to camp in a field it is obviously correct and courteous to obtain permission from the farmer or owner before attempting to pitch a tent or park a trailer-caravan.

The growing popularity of this form of holiday has ensured that there are today plenty of sites available and information on this score is readily obtainable from such sources as The Camping Club of Gt. Britain and Ireland, the two big motoring organisations (the R.A.C. and the A.A.), as well as some inexpensive publications giving details.

Motoring

A glance at the map will show that the road centres of East Anglia are King's Lynn, Norwich, Cambridge, Bury St. Edmunds, Ipswich and Colchester. Excellent roads link these centres, and almost every small town can be reached quickly by means of the major connecting roads. As a means of motoring from one centre to another, these major roads, as in other parts of the country, are the quickest and best routes. However, most of the interesting villages and most beautiful countryside lie 'off the beaten track' and on the narrow, winding lanes, where pleasant and unimpeded motoring is still possible within 100 miles of London if one plans the route carefully. Sections seven and ten of the AA three-miles-to-one-inch Touring Map by Geographia cover the entire area described in this guide.

For many the spring or early autumn are the best seasons in which to visit East Anglia. In the spring the countryside is bursting with new life, the green shows fresh and bright; in autumn the colours are at their richest, most particularly so in Breckland. Additionally, fewer holiday-makers are about at these times, accommodation is easier to obtain, and the roads considerably quieter. However, it should be remembered that roads leading to the ports are always busy.

WILDLIFE

ALTHOUGH EAST ANGLIA HAS LONG BEEN REGARDED as one of the best bird-watching areas in Great Britain we must be careful not to cover the area with one simple bland statement. Such is the terrain we must cover that one may be tempted to name it as the best 'reed-bed country', the 'best butterfly country', the 'best dragonfly country'. We may name its great sprawling Broads as almost tropical in appearance, or perhaps a second Holland. Indeed, East Anglia is all of these and more; a paradise for the naturalist and explorer. This country is for the nature-lover a place where each—botanist, ornithologist, or entomologist—may enjoy his own particular interest.

The Habitats

Here is a land of contrasts where man-made waterways merge into the slow, winding rivers of ages past. The rivers merge into shallow lagoons, swampland, fill a quarry-pit or spill into the mud-flats of the sea. Marshes, saltings, shingles, little creeks and coves contrast with flat arable pastures, orchards, woodland, dry heath and forest.

Simply to list the host of birds would make dull reading, such are the numbers involved. But refer to some we must, for they are an essential part of East Anglia. Bearded tits may be seen among the reeds, exotic spoonbills and even the delicate avocet. Great crested grebes cut a proud dash on the still waters. Hawks and harriers, once an exciting and expected sight, are now sadly rare. Heronries still survive and the boom of the bittern can now be heard once again on the broads of Minsmere.

WILDLIFE

Wildfowl

Wildfowl on the Ouse and Nene Washes are truly a wonderful sight. If you are impressed by sheer numbers then visit the Essex 'flats', where brent geese are to be seen in their thousands. Again, 'thousands' describes the flocks of knot which descend across the fertile feeding grounds of the Wash—January is the month to witness this spectacle. If your taste is for the rarity see the avocets in spring-time at Havergate Island, or the marsh harrier on Hickling Broad; see stone curlew breeding on the Suffolk coast and Breckland in June. Surprisingly, the red-legged partridge is more common than the native partridge.

Exotic Visitors

The tidal Stow sports one of the largest flocks of mute swans in the kingdom. Ducks are everywhere, particularly the mallard and shelduck, but gadwall, teal, shoveller, and the tufted duck are viewed in numbers in their season. Goosander, scaup, pintail, goldeneye are only a few of the visiting duck family. Turnstone, curlew, golden and grey plover, dunlin, sanderling, ringed plover, redshank and the lapwing wade in numbers everywhere along the coastline and waterways and the ruff is perhaps one of the waders we search for to see the display of its ruff. Lapwings are abundant and the gull family is seen everywhere. Cormorants appear much more numerous along the coastline than their close cousins the shag. Cley Marsh and Salthouse Heath are noted as one of the finest locations to view our waders of passage.

The Avocet

Indigenous Birds

But we must not restrict ourselves to the belief that great waterways are the only attraction. The nightingale sings, sandmartin, swallow and swift swoop through the sky, a few red-backed shrike may be searched for. Lesser and greater spotted woodpeckers drum in the woodlands. Spotted flycatchers dart about and wagtails bob on rocks, the tit family are well represented everywhere. That bright turquoise flash glimpsed only for a moment is, of course, none other than the kingfisher.

The thrush family, including the redwing and fieldfare, as well as the starling and skylark, arrive in the autumn in vast numbers.

Mammals

Of the mammals, the creature which has aroused the most interest in recent years must surely be the coypu (introduced from South America), whose activities are seriously undermining the banks of waterways. Its rapid spread throughout the Fens and Broads has caused the Ministry of Agriculture to take strong measures to check its progress. Escaped mink, too, have atrracted the attention of the Ministry.

Hedge Creatures

In the uplands of Cambridgeshire, parts of Norfolk and west Suffolk, foxes are plentiful; here and there rabbits are returning, but as yet they do not appear as common as the hare. Weasels haunt the hedgerows and rank growth, searching out bank and field voles, wood and house mice. The stoat unfortunately seems to be on the decline.

Badgers who dug their sets in the ancient mixed woodlands are now equally at home in the many coniferous plantations springing up here and there. A heavy toll is taken of the hedgehog as roads become busier. The shrew family, especially the pigmy, rush about in their frantic search for food, unseen, but with a small shrill voice. Moles leave their mark for everyone to see in neat 'heaves' or molehills so that we may have no doubt that they are there.

Grey squirrels steadily oust our native red, which everyone decries. Most of the bat family flit by night; the most numerous is perhaps the pipistrelle. A few harvest mice still survive the onslaught of mechanical farming.

The otter, too, steadily vanishes before civilisation.

Common frogs and toads are said to be declining and yet, strangely enough, edible frogs have appeared in odd places and may be spreading. Common lizards and smooth newts, slow-worms, grass snakes and the adder all add variety for the diligent searcher.

Lepidoptera

Here is a paradise for those interested in insect life, lowly midge, gay-coloured moth or beautiful butterflies. The largest butterfly, and perhaps the most beautiful of all, the swallowtail, flits across marsh and meadow. Across the waters we may find the most concentrated collection of dragonflies—half of the species recorded in Britain. Even the largest European dragonfly—the five-inch-spanned emperor—darts here and there in a shimmer of blue.

Search through rank on rank of reed splashed with the colour of lilies, or tread through drifts of pink willowherb. Perhaps you may peer through corn-cockle or toad flax in the cultivated fields. In Breckland, heather or grey lichen will cushion your feet. Bluebells and primrose garland the woodlands—wherever you go in your search for wildlife in East Anglia colour and birdsong will follow you.

GEOLOGY

GREAT BRITAIN IS PROBABLY UNIQUE in having such a variety of geological formations in so small a land area. In the extreme north-west highlands of Scotland we can view one of the most ancient of landscapes, the Lewisian Gneiss. These rocks vary in age from about 1,000 million to 3,000 million years which, seen in the context of current estimates of the age of the earth (4,500 million years), makes them extremely old.

Some of the rocks of East Anglia are, by comparison, hardly out of the womb. These are the very youngest to be seen in the British Isles, with an age of about one million years, decreasing to just a few years in the case of some of the beach deposits. The area of East Anglia is geologically quite distinctive from its neighbouring countryside. To the west are the remnants of the Fen country, now virtually drained, but when undrained provided a natural western boundary. To the south lies Essex, once heavily forested, and the Thames Basin, again geologically distinct as one moves from the unconsolidated deposits typical of East Anglia on to the London Clays of the Thames Basin. The whole area gives the impression of a gently undulating plateau dipping very gradually from the west to the coast in the east.

The Chalk

Basically, the 'foundation stone' of East Anglia is the Cretaceous Chalk. This is the oldest rock type to be found in the area, with an approximate age of 100 million years. The chalk forms a subdued outcrop, occurring in the north between Hunstanton, Scolt Head and Weybourne, and dipping due south towards the London Basin, where it becomes covered by the more recent London Clay deposits. The East Anglian Chalk provides a much more subdued topography than its neighbouring chalk areas, because it alone was subjected to smoothing glacial action.

One can appreciate the gentleness of the dip of the chalk from the fact that at Norwich the top of it is at about fifty feet above sea-level, whereas at Yarmouth, on the coast, it is covered by 500 feet of more recent deposits. This chalk surface is an eroded one, in that, after the deposition of the chalk, some of the topmost layers were eroded to give the existing surface.

Scenically, the Cretaceous landscape of present-day East Anglia is very similar to other chalk areas in the British Isles, albeit on a smaller scale. One can still see the same type of rolling downs with typically short grass around Newmarket. Slight cliffs are also formed on the coast around Hunstanton in the north.

Flint

Flint has been mined from the chalk in the western areas around Brandon and can often be seen used as a building stone. Originally the use of flint for stonemasonry was a case of necessity because of the lack of any suitable alternative stone. This has resulted in a variety of flint workmanship, from fairly crude examples on earlier buildings where the rough flint was simply bonded with a mortar, to more recent examples, particularly churches, where the flint is actually worked. The villages of Kelling, Trimingham and Weybourne in the north, near Cromer, are noted for their use of flint in many of their cottages. Cromer church itself is also a fine example of the use of dressed flint. The church at Southwold and the old Guildhall of Norwich are also worthy of note. Flint gravels, quarried locally, are used as a road-stone in the area. The light brown roads reflect the typical colour of these flint gravels.

Glaciers in East Anglia

Although the chalk is a considerable part of the East Anglian countryside, it is not the rock type for which the area is best known. There are, in fact, the glacial deposits, which are exhibited here on a more comprehensive scale than anywhere else in Britain.

Immediately prior to the Great Ice Age, the chalk deposits were covered by a series of unconsolidated estuarine sands, muds and gravels, dumped over the eastern area by the combined action of the Thames and Rhine. At that time these two major rivers had joined forces in the southern half of what is, today, the North Sea, to flow northwards. It is these deposits, known collectively as the 'Crag', which bore the first brunt of the ice advance. They extend more or less eastward from a line through Weybourne south by Norwich to Ipswich. Thus, when one visits, for example, the Lake District, or the Highlands of Scotland, there one is seeing the results of the same natural agents exercising themselves on a completely different environment, namely unconsolidated river and estuarine deposits.

Contorted Drift

Large glaciers moved into East Anglia from the north, and the result of this ice movement is twofold. Firstly, considerable abrasive energy is brought to bear on the underlying bedrock. In the highland areas of Britain evidence of the passage of a glacier can be seen in the smooth 'U'-shaped valleys, the striated boulders and

many other familiar features. In East Anglia, however, the effect is
different because the ice moved over an area of loose deposits. This
movement often caused the underlying material to contort into
complex thrust-type folds, giving rise to the phenomena of 'contorted
drift'. Examples of this contortion can be seen in the Cromer Ridge
in the north, particularly in the sea-cliffs, and also in the Ipswich
neighbourhood at Claydon and Hadleigh Road.

Boulder Clay

As well as affecting pre-existing material, the encroachment of
glaciers over an area inevitably results in the deposition of a variety
of morainic deposits. Much of this loose boulder clay, in the case of
East Anglia, is locally derived, but some Scandinavian rock fragments
can be found. Not surprisingly, a large amount of chalk debris has
been incorporated into the various boulder clays, so much so that
they are sometimes referred to as Chalky Boulder Clay. Indeed, so
much chalk became incorporated in the boulder clay around Holt and
Weybourne, that it was actually quarried for lime.

During an Ice Age, it is quite common for an area to be swept by
a succession of glaciers, each indicative of a climatic fluctuation.
Evidence for such fluctuations can certainly be detected in East
Anglia, indicating a total of four seperate glaciations.

The first occasion brought in ice from the North Sea, and is
called, appropriately, the North Sea Glaciation. During this period,
loamy material was deposited in the general area between Sheringham,
Norwich and Yarmouth. This part of Norfolk rarely exceeds fifty feet
in height, and is altogether quite featureless, except for the Broads.

The second glacial episode, known as the Great Eastern Glacier,
was considerably more extensive, and brought with it the Chalky
Boulder Clay, as well as copious amounts of sand and gravel.

The Cromer Ridge

The Little Eastern Glacier, the third in the series, was responsible
for the 300-foot-high Cromer Ridge in north Norfolk. This is one of
the best examples of a morainic deposit. The Cromer Ridge is
composed of a whole series of small ridges, all more or less parallel.
Each one represents a fluctuation, or a period of hesitancy, in the
retreat of the glacier. One can appreciate that, if the front of a glacier
remains stationary, a large amount of debris carried on and within the
glacier will accumulate at this point. This is, in fact, how a moraine
is formed. If then the glacier 'retreats', say, a quarter of a mile and
then remains stationary for a further time-span, a second morainic
deposit will form, similar in almost every respect to the first. One can
envisage a combination of such circumstances building up one very
large moraine, and this is exactly how the Cromer Ridge was
formed.

The fourth glaciation was very slight, barely impinging on the
Norfolk coast.

There is quite a variety of types of unconsolidated deposits covering East Anglia, a variety often reflected quite accurately in the distribution of different vegetation regimes. For example, where the drift is of a dominantly loamy character, and therefore very fertile, extensive cornfields have developed.

The Breckland

By contrast, where the drift is composed almost exclusively of sand and gravel, a heathland type of countryside develops, often typically with a thriving conifer population. Perhaps the most notable heath-type area in East Anglia is that known as the Breckland, approximately 300–400 square miles straddling the Norfolk and Suffolk border around the town of Thetford. Before the Forestry Commission embarked on this very large afforestation programme, Breckland was an expanse of land very similar to the steppes of central Europe. It is an area of heathland, with poor soils, quite unsuitable for cultivation. Because of the porosity of the soil, water is a scarce commodity, which is another reason for the lack of human settlement in the area. These heathlands provide a striking contrast to the more fertile loamy soils.

The Broads

This complex network of intertwined waterways, situated in flat meadowland, has managed to withhold the complete story of its origin. However, the most likely explanation suggests that after the land subsided during the Neolithic Submerged Forest Period, about 3,000 B.C., the river valleys which now contain the Broads became submerged. Instead of becoming saline estuaries, powerful longshore drift of sediment along the coast dammed up these drowned valleys and they soon became freshwater ponds. The Broads are, of course, very shallow, and even now are being slowly silted up, as witness the flat, waterlogged, reed-bordered meadows adjacent to these stretches of water.

The Fens

The Fens are not strictly part of East Anglia, being more of a boundary area than an integral part. Nevertheless, the very subdued topography of the Fens is reminiscent of many parts of East Anglia, and therefore worthy of attention here.

The Fenlands themselves reach southwards from the Wash towards Cambridge, and are composed essentially of flat-lying peat and silt deposits. Occasional 'islands' of solid rock, or more frequently, boulder clay, rise above the general land surface. These latter phenomena are a reminder of the effects of the Ice Age. Human settlement has frequently taken advantage of these relative high spots, notably at Boston and Ely. These places provided valuable sanctuary for early human settlers, and continued to do so right into historic times: in this context one has only to recall the stand made by Hereward the Wake against the invading Normans.

GEOLOGY

This area of the country was originally a large sea inlet, in fact a southerly extension of the Wash. This sea eventually became filled with a combination of marine detritus and river silts. Marsh and swamp vegetation flourished, encouraging the silting process, until finally a waterlogged, but extremely fertile, area appeared. One can still see the remnants of this marine incursion in the typical marine sands and gravels which outcrop the periphery of the Fenlands. So fertile is this ground that considerable time and energy was expended in draining the Fens. Today, with almost the whole area under cultivation, the population per acre is the highest in Britain for an agricultural district.

The Coast

Perhaps the final comment on East Anglia can be directed towards the coastline, a truly splendid example of dynamic geological forces in action. As the reader will now appreciate, the vast majority of East Anglia is composed of soft, unconsolidated deposits, and these of course are easy prey to vigorous marine action such as the North Sea can provide. The North Sea is, in fact, one of the roughest, most unpredictable weather areas in the world and frequently the coast of East Anglia bears the brunt of the worst of this weather. It is therefore not surprising to find that this coastline is in fact the fastest changing part of the British countryside.

Marshes

The most obvious signs of coastal activity can be seen in the often very extensive spits developed across rivermouths. Longshore drift at Yarmouth and also at Aldeburgh has moved the mouths of the rivers Yare and Alde considerable distances downstream from their original entry points into the North Sea. The River Alde, for example, approaches the sea just south of Aldeburgh, then is deflected southwards for a distance of about eleven miles before entering the sea. The narrow zone of land between river and sea is one of marsh, composed mainly of sand, gravel and shingle. This is a common feature of the East Anglian coast and is due as much to wave and wind action as to tidal movement. Perhaps the most interesting feature of this longshore drift is that it changes direction at one point on the coast. To the east of Blakeney, near Cromer, drift movement is towards the east and south, but west of Blakeney the movement of beach material is towards the west.

Erosion

In some places, notably on the northern coast, erosion of the soft cliffs is so rapid that the loose deposits have not even had time enough to slump. Possibly the best known example of coastal erosion concerns the destruction of the church at Eccles, north of Yarmouth. When this building was first erected it was separated from the sea by an expanse of sand-dunes. In time these dunes began to encroach inland until they eventually buried the church. A little later the church appeared on the seaward side of the dunes, as though awaiting Nature's last onslaught—by the sea itself. Within a hundred years the church had been completely destroyed by marine erosion.

Bibliography

This has, of necessity, been a brief description of the geology of East Anglia. For a more detailed account the reader is referred to the *British Regional Geology of East Anglia*, published by the Geological Survey, and available in all government stationery shops. Much time can be spent amongst the Crags and other loose deposits, hunting for fossils. Those interested are recommended to obtain a copy of the British Museum's publication on recent fossils: this is a small pocket-size booklet with numerous excellent drawings to facilitate identification. Finally, J. A. Steers, in his text *The Coastline of England and Wales*, includes a comprehensive section on the coast of East Anglia.

ENGLISH TOURIST BOARD

A network of Tourist Information Centres exists throughout England. Each displays a sign, a red Tudor rose with the words 'Tourist Information' on a blue ground. This is the symbol of the English Tourist Information Services.

Centres are categorised as follows:

NATIONAL (N)   which give information on every part of England.

REGIONAL (R)   offices which deal with the Tourist Board region in which they are located.

LOCAL (L)   where the staff answer only questions concerning purely local interest.

SPECIALISED (S) centres where details on particular subjects, National Parks, The National Trust etc., are available.

Addresses of these offices are quoted in this Guide. Many centres maintain a Tourist Accommodation Service—available to personal callers only. This is indicated thus:

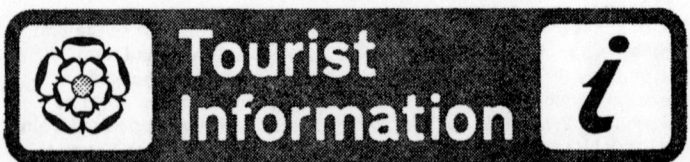

Section 2　　　　Norfolk Coast

KING'S LYNN

Population: 30,000
Early Closing Day: Wednesday
Market Days: Tuesday/Saturday
Tourist Information (R) Town Hall
　　　　　　　　　　　Saturday Market Place 🛏

THERE WAS A TIME when most of the Fen streams flowed into the sea some miles south of the present site of King's Lynn, probably where the town of Wisbech is today; whether at that time there was a port of King's Lynn cannot with certainty be said. By the twelfth and thirteenth centuries the estuary of these streams, the Wash, had commenced silting up, the River Great Ouse had changed its course sufficiently to allow King's Lynn to grow and quickly become one of the great ports of the country.

Royal Charter

It was in the very early years of the twelfth century that Bishop Herbert de Losinga of Norwich built the church of St. Margaret and the Priory which adjoined it. A hundred years later King John visited the town and, finding that the port dues were only one-third less than those of London, granted Lynn a Royal Charter making it a free borough with a number of other privileges. By the fourteenth century, Lynn had become a very prosperous port, King Henry III had the Great Ouse diverted and the estuary deepened and widened thus taking the first steps in the centuries-long battle to reclaim the Fenlands, and the salt marshes of the coastal areas.

Fourth City

By the early eighteenth century the value of corn exported from Lynn exceeded a quarter of a million pounds and in imports of wine and coal the city came fourth in the country, after London, Bristol and Newcastle. The rivers provided the best means of transport for goods to the Midlands and the south of England. By 1750 the mail and passenger coaches were operating between King's Lynn and London and the port's prosperity grew apace. In 1847 the railway arrived, then followed the steamers and the modern port of King's Lynn began to take shape.

Fisher Fleet

Today this is an ever-expanding port and town, for the old advantages still hold good. The annual turnover of imports and exports tops 250,000 tons and includes such varied items as petroleum products, bulk grain, chemicals, timber, motor-cars, flower bulbs and agricultural machinery in addition to general cargoes. The waterway connecting the two great docks, the Alexandra and the Bentinck, is known as the Fisher Fleet and here Lynn's quite considerable fishing fleet lands its cargoes of whitefish, cod, shrim'p and shellfish. As long ago as the fourteenth century boats from King s Lynn were fishing in the northern seas.

Encouraging Outlook

King's Lynn is one of the few industrial centres in an almost completely agricultural county. The manufacture and processing of chemicals, fertilisers and stock feed, farm machinery and the thousand and one items that are called for in modern agriculture, account for quite a considerable part of Lynn's industrial life. Engineering, timber

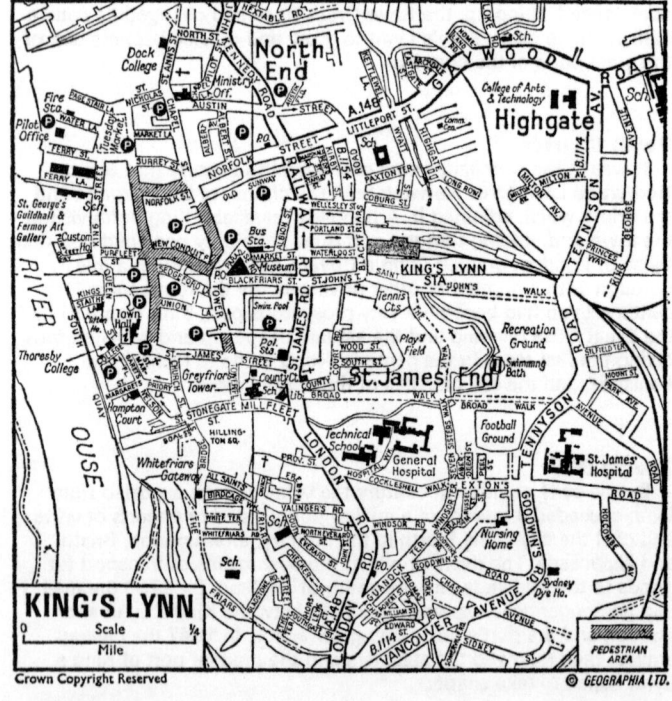

KING'S LYNN

and a host of varied and diverse industries, appear to assure a prosperity far into the future for Lynn's industrial population.

Historic Heritage

There is another side to the life of this ancient port in which the visitor may be particularly interested. Few towns of comparable size have done more to preserve their worthy monuments of the past, and Lynn has, perhaps, more than most. The following are some of the most important and worth-while of the many ancient buildings and monuments.

St. Margaret's is the parish church of King's Lynn and dominates the scene of the Saturday market. Built in the twelfth century, its twin towers are all that remain of the original structure. One of these was surmounted by a spire, but in the eighteenth century it fell, and it was at this time that reconstruction took place and much of the Norman work disappeared. There is a chancel with a thirteenth-century arcade and a fine fifteenth-century clerestory above. The present building is largely Early English and Perpendicular and in the interior perhaps most interesting are the Flemish brasses, the choir-stalls and the lectern.

All Saints' Church, off Friars Street, is largely fourteenth century, with a notable painted rood-screen and some fine carving in aisle roofs. Note the anchor-hold, the cell in which women hermits lived between the thirteenth and fifteenth centuries.

St. Nicholas' Chapel, which was rebuilt in 1419; note the fifteenth-century lectern and other woodwork of the same date, also the magnificent 'Angel Roof' and the large west window with eleven lights.

The Red Mount Chapel, a three-storeyed building of 1485, is supposed to have been used by pilgrims on journeys to Walsingham; note the fan-vaulted roof. The key can be obtained from the Catholic Presbytery.

Town Walls

The South Gate is near the southern entrance to Lynn and has to be passed through on the journey from the south; this has been the case since 1520, when it was rebuilt. It was then part of the town walls. Close by are the remains of the entrance gateway to the Carmelite, or Whitefriars, Monastery. A little farther north is the Greenland Fishery, which was built in 1605 as a residence; in the eighteenth century it became an inn frequented by whaler crews, thus the name. In 1941 it was damaged by bombing, but has been restored; it is occupied as offices.

Hampton Court is another interesting and ancient residence. The south wing, originally built in the thirteenth century, was rebuilt in the fourteenth for a wealthy merchant. The west wing was added in the fifteenth century, while the east and north wings came in the sixteenth and seventeenth centuries. This is, so far as the south wing is concerned, one of the oldest residences in the country.

Hanseatic Link

Nearby is St. Margaret's Lane, which houses a very remarkable set of warehouses dating from 1428 which were the property of the Hanseatic League, a famous German and Scandinavian merchant combine that was extremely powerful in the thirteenth and fourteenth centuries; it was known as the Steelyard.

Clifton House in Queen Street is another fine example of a wealthy merchant's house; of fourteenth-century origin with a fine and complete entrance, it is open to the public during office hours; in the crypt are traces of a twelfth-century building. The Elizabethan brick watch-tower, the tile floors with brick surrounds, the fine panelling and plasterwork, make this a most attractive and worth-while visit.

Guildhalls

On the east side of Queen Street is the Guildhall of The Holy Trinity; today it is the Town Hall and Council Offices, which are, of course, open to the public. This truly magnificent structure was rebuilt in 1421 and matches in date of origin so many of the loveliest remaining buildings in Lynn. Farther north, off King Street, is the Guildhall of St. George, which is supposed to be the oldest example of a medieval Merchant Guild. It is of fifteenth-century origin and during the eighteenth century was used as a theatre; it now serves as a centre for the King's Lynn Festival held each year in July. It is open to the public and is the property of the National Trust.

There are many other buildings of interest and beauty of which the Custom House of 1683 is, perhaps, the most impressive. A stroll should be taken along Nelson Street, Queen Street and King Street, also around the Tuesday market, where the Duke's Head Hotel, dating from 1685, should be seen. St. Nicholas' Chapel and St. Nicholas Street will reveal more old and fascinating buildings, as will a return along the medieval waterfront. King's Lynn is a place that will well repay a thorough exploration by those interested in architecture or historical buildings.

Lively Markets

As a shopping centre King's Lynn stands quite alone, for there is no other town of comparable size within a radius of forty miles. The two markets, the Saturday market at the south end, and the Tuesday market at the north end of High Street, which is itself the main shopping street, offer a selection of old-established family shops and modern supermarkets that should please the most value-conscious housewife. In addition there are side streets where many of the older shops, such as saddlers, basketmakers and antique dealers are housed.

King's Lynn is well equipped with parks and recreation grounds, of which The Walks, where the Red Mount Chapel will be found, must be counted the nicest. Of the many famous figures that were born in or are connected with King's Lynn, a few must be mentioned. Captain George Vancouver was born in what is now

New Conduit Street in 1757: at fourteen years of age he sailed with Captain Cook on his second voyage of discovery; in 1790 he commanded an expedition searching for the North-west Passage between the Atlantic and the Pacific, during the course of which he sailed right around Vancouver Island and charted the west coast of North America.

Virginia

The state of Virginia owes a great deal to three Lynn men: Captain John Smith, John Rolfe and William Clabourne. These three were among the very early settlers and William Clabourne was the first Secretary of State of Virginia.

Salt Marshes

The boundary with Lincolnshire is some eight miles west of King's Lynn by the coast road. This piece of country is known as agricultural marshland; absolutely flat, extremely fertile and producing market-garden produce, it is the direct result of the reclamation of the ancient salt-marshes. A drive along the narrow road from Terrington St. Clement to the sea wall at Ongar Hill will provide one of the best views possible of the wild and un-reclaimed salt-marshes on the seaward side of the wall while *en route* one can obtain a full appreciation of the tremendous fertility of this once useless tract of land, and some appreciation of the time and effort required for this reclamation.

Unusual Churches

The village of Terrington St. Clement is itself of little interest as, with most of the marsh and fen villages, it is fully occupied with its daily work. However, the church, dedicated to St. Clement, has often been called the Cathedral of the Marshes and it undoubtedly deserves the title. The west end and the south side are by far the most impressive, with the great square tower on the north side of the west front. Most of the present church is Perpendicular, fifteenth century, but there are some details which recall the thirteenth century, when this magnificent village church was first built. Note the large number of clerestory windows, the arrangement of the south transept windows, the font, with a most unusual wood cover, the bottom portion of which opens to reveal painted landscapes. St. Clement's is cruciform in style and no doubt was intended to have a central tower. Combined with the drive to the sea wall, a visit to St. Clement's makes a very well-worth-while excursion from King's Lynn.

North of King's Lynn the marshes hug the coast while the road follows the heath, the narrow northern end of the Breckland, which is well wooded and quite beautiful in its own particular way. The church at South Wooton, a little north of King's Lynn, is perhaps worth a visit to see the font, which is Norman, with a square bowl standing on nine pillars with some very strange decorations. The bier is dated 1611 and again is most unusual.

Tudor Almshouse

Castle Rising, the next little village, is most un-twentieth century in appearance. There is some new building, but the general impression is of red Tudor brick and red pantiles under a cover of fine trees. The most outstanding building is The Trinity Hospital, which was built in the sixteenth or very early seventeenth century by the Earl of Northampton, owner of Castle Rising. Today it is an almshouse for old ladies and, in red Tudor brick, is one of the most charming of buildings. The chapel was rebuilt in 1807 but the original furniture was re-installed. It is said that the original furniture is still in use by the old ladies in their living-quarters.

Castle Rising

The church of St. Lawrence is late Norman but has been almost entirely rebuilt; there are several interesting Norman remains of which the very richly ornamented font is perhaps the best. Nearby, the Dept. of Environment control the deeply moated Castle Rising, which is a splendid example of the Norman Keep and is similar in some respects to Norwich Castle. Almost square, it is somewhat broader than its height, giving an impression of great strength. Entry is made over a fifteenth-century bridge across the ditch or moat and, although the Keep is roofless and floorless over the central area, a great deal remains, and the walls are more or less complete. In a county where castles are somewhat rare, Castle Rising should not be missed.

Sandringham

About three miles north of Castle Rising is the Royal Estate of Sandringham, which is open to the public on most days during the summer months when the Royal Family is not in residence. Sandringham House, country home of the Queen is open similarly.

There is no village of Sandringham, the parish church being within the walled park, and anyone may attend the services provided there is room after the parishioners are seated. It was a simple little church, but has been so decorated and enriched by the Royal Family since 1857 that it is now to all intents Victorian. With its royal connections it is, however, of some interest, and contains a number of beautiful pieces of church furniture. The real attraction and glory of Sandringham is the surrounding heath- and forest-land.

Wolferton Station

The former 'Royal Retiring Rooms' have been preserved and may now be seen by the public during the summer months. Built in 1898 for the exclusive use of Kings and Queens and royal guests visiting

Sandringham, the panelling and gold fittings are very handsome. There are also delightful relics of Edwardian railway journeys plus old posters.

Elizabethan Barn

Dersingham, the next village, was a pretty little place of red brick, but new building has somewhat spoiled the overall effect. Southwards is the attractive heathland, while towards the west the marshes stretch to the sea. The church of St. Nicholas is fourteenth century slightly altered in the fifteenth. The most interesting item is a beautifully carved wooden chest of the fourteenth or fifteenth century; there are several other interesting pieces of furniture.

Next door to the church is an Elizabethan barn with the date 1672. Built of stone and hand-made bricks with stepped gables, it is a fascinating relic of past days, and is still in use.

Sanctuary Bell

Three miles farther north is the little village of Snettisham; while there is little of great interest the variety and character of the buildings are more attractive than in many villages in north-west Norfolk. The fourteenth-century church, however, is a very fine example of the Decorated style. It has a spire over 170 feet in height. The chancel has gone, so that now the once central tower is at the east end. Note the narthex, or triple-arched portico, at the west end above which is the magnificent window of six lights. The inside should be viewed from east to west, towards the great window. Note also the thirteenth-century sanctuary bell with the original fixings on to a wooden axle; this is one of very few left in the country.

Lavender Fields

About halfway between Snettisham and the town of Hunstanton is the village of Heacham, which lies between the main road, the A149, and the sea. From the holiday-maker's point of view, Heacham is one huge caravan camp, with a limitless beach on which there are a number of notices warning the swimmer to be careful. Caley Mill, close to the village, is Victorian in the Tudor style and is the hub of a lavender industry; the surrounding fields are, when the lavender is in flower, a most attractive picture with a delightful scent.

HUNSTANTON

Population: 5,000

Tourist Information (R) Le Strange Terrace

HUNSTANTON ST. EDMUND, OR NEW HUNSTANTON, is immediately south of the village known as Old Hunstanton. Although situated on the east coast of England, Hunstanton faces west across the Wash and so misses many of the east winds. While New Hunstanton developed largely towards the end of the nineteenth century, Old Hunstanton has been there at least since Norman times.

Attractive Beach

The seemingly endless and very safe sandy beach is one of the greatest attractions; add to this the very beautiful gardens and greens, the cliff-top walks, the lovely surrounding countryside, the endless sports and amusements fostered by an energetic council, and Hunstanton adds up to a very popular resort. Aquatic sports, sailing and fishing are well catered for and there is a sailing school and frequent yacht races.

Coloured Cliffs

North of the pier the cliffs rise to fifty or so feet, topped with green grass, then a foot or so of white chalk, then a layer of brown carstone with whitish scree at the foot, then the brown sands and the greenish sea make a colour scheme on a sunny day that is little short of surprising and an extremely attractive backcloth.

Old Lighthouse

At Old Hunstanton there is a disused lighthouse attached to a private residence, and nearby, in a public garden, the scant ruins of St. Edmund's Chapel. The parish church of St. Mary towers above the old village. It is a fine example of the use of flint, and, although considerably altered last century, it contains a number of interesting features, more particularly of the Le Strange family who, in addition to having been largely responsible for the early development of New Hunstanton, have lived there since the fifteenth century.

Rare Birds

Although so much of the coast on either side of Hunstanton is sand backed by low cliffs, there are nearby marshes where the ornithologist and naturalist may pursue his interests because the roads to these outlying marshes are infrequently used and many rare birds can be seen.

Nature Reserves

About seven miles east of Hunstanton is the tiny village of Titchwell, with our first example of the round-towered church constructed of flint and stone. Some more examples of round towers and a vast amount of flint-building will be seen in both Norfolk and Suffolk. At Brancaster the National Trust own over 2,000 acres of the foreshore and marshes which are opposite Scolt Head, an offshore island which also belongs to the National Trust; both these extensive properties are nature reserves. A narrow road, which at high tide is under water, leads to the beach. At Brancaster Staithe transport to Scolt Head can be obtained on application to Mr. R. Chestney, Dial House, Brancaster.

The Burnhams

A little cluster of Burnhams comes next; of these Burnham Market is the most important. It is a village with a very long green surrounded with Georgian houses and little changed since the eighteenth century. The church of St. Mary, Burnham Westgate, has a square tower and is quite an imposing edifice. From Burnham Deepdale, which is three miles from Burnham Market, a middle-distance view can be had of Scolt Head. Here the round tower of flint and stone appears again in the village church. At Burnham Norton, red brick and black flints are the outstanding impression; it is in sight of the sea with a very beautiful little church on a small hilltop nearer Burnham Market; here is another round tower of flint and stone.

Burnham Overy is perhaps the loveliest of all the Burnhams; its near neighbour Overy Staithe has a little harbour on a creek a long way from the sea; about an acre of pasture in the middle of the village has been taken over by the National Trust who have also acquired the Burnham Overy Water Mill and Maltings. Burnham Overy itself has a small green with a cottage whose doorway is framed with four white busts; there are also the remains of a Market Cross and a very unusual Norman church.

Birthplace of Nelson

Burnham Thorpe, as the birthplace of Admiral Lord Nelson, deserves especial mention. That great seaman was born in the Rectory in 1758; this house was demolished a long while ago but a plaque beside the road marks the site. The local inn is of course the Lord Nelson. Many mementos of the Admiral are housed in the church, which dates from the thirteenth century. On special feast days a replica of the flag flown on the *Victory* at the Battle of Trafalgar is flown from the church. The Burnhams have changed very little since Nelson spent his boyhood here.

Holkham Hall

Holkham Hall, the Norfolk home of the Earls of Leicester, and built by Sir Edward Coke, the first Earl, is one of those outstanding places that must not be missed. The park is a restful expanse of timbered grassland that was a waste of sand in the eighteenth century. The Hall is magnificent both inside and out. A Palladian mansion, in the style of an Italian palace of the period, it was built between 1734 and 1759. The front measures 340 feet and has a magnificent central portico. The inside is lavish in the extreme; all the main rooms, including the ceilings, tapestries, paintings, etc., are magnificent in the eighteenth-century manner. Viewed from the north the outside has a distinctly severe appearance, but from the south it is little short of dramatic, for one approaches from a slightly higher level and sees the splendid and eminently graceful front against the background of the lake, the trees and extensive parkland. Holkham Hall is open to the public at certain times but the park is open on most days.

'Turnip' Townsend

It is, however, the agricultural history behind this great Hall and the 25,000 acres of the estate that should be of the greatest interest to the country. In 1776 the great nephew of the builder of Holkham, known as 'Coke of Norfolk', succeeded to this vast estate and promptly set about improving the output of the very poor and sandy lands. No wheat was grown at this time and the stocking of sheep was very low indeed. Two tenants, who refused to pay a higher rent, left, and Coke decided to work these two farms himself. He tried many innovations and experiments, utilised the knowledge gained some years earlier by 'Turnip' Townsend and eventually evolved the system of four-course rotation which, until the Second World War, was the basis of English mixed arable farming. It is of this great service to agriculture that one is reminded when viewing the great mansion and the adjoining park.

Ancient Harbour

Three miles east of Holkham is the pleasant little resort of Wells-next-the-Sea. This ancient little harbour was known as Guella in Domesday Book and, although never assuming greatness, it has always been a fairly prosperous little port. Situated on a wide creek about a mile from the sea this harbour is particularly safe. Fertilisers are the chief import and a small fishing fleet still operates. The harbour area is a very pleasant mixture of old and new. A straight road leads to the sea wall and the sands which at low tide stretch out for about a mile; here there is the lifeboat station, rows of beach huts, car parks and caravan site. The adjacent marshes provide some first-class wildfowling. In Church Plain there are some nice Georgian houses and the church of St. Nicholas, which was completely rebuilt in 1879 after a fire; inside there is a remarkable wooden chest dated 1635.

Stiffkey

The little village of Stiffkey, built almost entirely of flint and brick, is about four miles east of Wells. The church of St. John the Baptist is also largely of flint and brick; it was originally built in the thirteenth or fourteenth century but has suffered some rebuilding since. Stiffkey Hall, of the middle sixteenth century, is partly in ruins; the ruins of the great hall and the four round towers, of flint and brick, make an odd picture against the nearby church.

Some seven miles east of Wells is the tiny harbour of Blakeney

BLAKENEY POINT

that once, when the sea was a great deal nearer, was a commercial port; today it is a haven for yachts and small fishing vessels on the estuary of the Glaven. Pleasant flint-built houses, the fifteenth-century church with an outstanding tower and the nearby beacon tower, miles of marshes and winding creeks with the all-pervading atmosphere of the sea, make of Blakeney a more than pleasant, if quiet, resort for the yachtsman and the wildfowler. Blakeney Point, which is a National Trust Nature Reserve, stretches for five miles from the village of Cley to well west of Blakeney; it is a narrow strip of sand and shingle enclosing the estuary of the Glaven and is regarded as a site for the study of the action of the sea as well as a breeding ground for sea birds, particularly various terns.

Tower Windmill

The very pretty little village of Cley-next-the-Sea sits comfortably on the east bank of the River Glaven. Prior to the seventeenth century, before the estuary had silted up, Cley was a quite important port; land reclamation combined with this natural silting finally destroyed the ports of Cley and nearby Salthouse. The most outstanding feature of Cley is the Tower Windmill and among the other notable features are many small and attractive flint houses, the Georgian custom house and the Maison de Quay with a fifteenth-century doorway. The beach is at the end of a long, narrow road and here there is a coastguard lookout, a shelter and car park. There are extensive marshes on either hand. Salthouse Broad is National Trust property.

St. Margaret's Church at the southern end of the village is a splendid building in some ways. It is the south side that deserves the adjective 'splendid' for the rest is far more commonplace; there are several sixteenth-century brasses and other interesting furnishings.

Former Ports

On the opposite bank of the River Glaven from Cley stands the little village of Wiveton; it has an interesting history. Less than two hundred years ago the green meadows on both banks of the river between the two villages were a tidal estuary, both villages had harbours and from both ships sailed to the Continent. From the churchyard at Wiveton a very fine view can be had of the surrounding country, including Cley. The little church of St. Mary is a fourteenth-century building and is exceptionally interesting. Nearby is a medieval bridge of one arch with five ribs. Salthouse has a lonely little fifteenth-century church and once had a small port which was ruined by the land reclamation of the eighteenth century. There is a considerable area of marsh towards the sea but a good beach over the sea wall.

At Weybourne, the next little village, the sea wall ends and the low cliffs take charge. It is a nice, tiny resort without any of the modern embellishments. There is a fourteenth-century priory and church of All Saints with the tower remaining from a previous Anglo-Saxon church. West and south-west are the heathlands, well supplied with paths and wooded roads where the walker may feel at home. Weybourne also has a good beach.

Coast Walk

The road from Weybourne to Sheringham runs through some extraordinarily pretty country, while the coast walk along the cliff-top is to be recommended.

SHERINGHAM

Population: 5,500
Early Closing Day: Wednesday
Market Day: Saturday
Tourist Information: (R) Station Road (summer only)

SHERINGHAM IS QUITE SIMPLY A SEASIDE RESORT and a very pleasant one. It consists of two villages that have grown into one town; the old fishing village, with hundreds of years of history behind it, is the more enjoyable of the two; Upper Sheringham, on the hill, was an agricultural village and is now the residential quarter. Sheringham is an excellent shopping centre and has most of the amenities expected of a modern resort. Although there is a little shingle the sands are clean and extensive.

The church of All Saints in Upper Sheringham is most worth a visit from the architectural viewpoint. The tower is thirteenth century, the arcades are fourteenth, while the clerestory is probably of the same date.

Fishing is possible from the beach and boats are available for expeditions further out to sea.

Coastal Defences

It was not until the end of the last century that the fishing village of Sheringham commenced to welcome visitors and became something of a resort; from then the growth of this little place became phenomenal but fortunately a great deal of the old fishing village atmosphere remains. During the eighteenth and nineteenth centuries considerable coast erosion took place, the old Crown Hotel was washed into the sea, but coast defences have halted this and Sheringham now enjoys a beach fairly safe from erosion.

Cliff Walks

There are many very pleasant walks in the vicinity; one of the nicest is along the coast and cliffs to Cromer, a little over three miles. East of Sheringham the coast is alternately low cliffs and sandy stretches, but a few miles westwards towards Cley and Wells, the marshes commence and walkers should exercise considerable care. From the trig:point on the cliffs to the east of the town a very fine view of the whole of Sheringham can be had; particularly attractive is the view of the red-roofed flint-built houses and cottages of the old fishing village.

Railway Museum

Housed at the now disused railway station is one of those rare exhibitions of the steam-engines of a past era in railway travel. The North Norfolk Railway Company has a number of steam-engines and coaches from the early years of this century on show, and has opened for passenger traffic the line between Weybourne and Sheringham; it is also hoped that, at a later date, the line will be re-laid and traffic re-established as far as Holt. The present exhibition at the old Sheringham station should not be missed.

The exhibition is open daily during the summer, and trains run at weekends and holidays May to October.

CROMER

Population: 5,500
Early Closing Day: Wednesday
Tourist Information: (R) North Lodge Park (summer only)

CROMER IS UNDOUBTEDLY ONE OF THE NICEST of Norfolk's seaside resorts. It is situated in the hilly part of the county and, although these hills nowhere rise to more than 300 feet, they do add contrast and variety to the scene. On either side of the town the cliffs are wild, fascinating and the home of myriads of sea birds.

High Tower

The most outstanding feature of the town is the tower of the parish church of St. Peter and St. Paul; it is 160 feet tall and by far the highest in Norfolk.

At one time this tower was in use as a lighthouse, a lantern then being used to show the necessary warning light.

Cliff-top Gardens

The town is not only a good shopping centre but a remarkably pleasant place, while the front and the beach, with cliff-top gardens and steps winding down to the sands, should please most holiday-makers. Essentially it is a quieter resort than some, and the lack of old buildings enhances the many Victorian villas which have been turned, in many cases, into hotels. The small and elegant cottages near the church have remained, intensifying the height and strength of the church tower.

Famous Lifeboat

Cromer was, and in a way still is, an historic fishing village famed for its lifeboat and its even more famous coxswain, Henry Blogg, who commanded it from 1909 to 1947 winning the R.N.L.I. gold medal three times, in addition to other decorations. At eighteen years old he was a member of the crew of the rowing and sailing lifeboat. The north Norfolk coast can be very dangerous to shipping and the fishermen of these parts are among the most skilled small-boat men.

Nature Park

It was not until late last century that Cromer really began to develop as a resort. Now the process has been accelerated by the decline in the fishing industry; some boats still fish from Cromer, largely for crabs, etc., and it is the fishermen who make up the crews for the two lifeboats, one of which is launched from the pier. It is this pier that provides so much of the entertainment for visitors. A mile west of the town is the very delightful Nature Park, close to the sea and in very beautiful surroundings, with many exotic birds and animals. The lighthouse at the east end of the town is often open to the public.

On leaving Cromer for the south the A149 strikes inland to North Walsham and Great Yarmouth, while a narrower, and perhaps more pleasant, road continues to skirt the coast, visiting a number of quite small villages and seaside resorts before rejoining the A149 at Caister-on-Sea.

Good Beaches

The first of these villages is Overstrand, about two miles from Cromer and stretching from the main road to the cliffs and the extensive beach of clean sand. Steps lead down to the beach from the cliffs. There is a promenade along the sea wall. The shallow sea and clean sand make this a good place for small children. The church of St. Martin was built in the fourteenth century but has since been much rebuilt; it has a round tower with an ancient oven for baking, probably for the sacrament. A little farther south is Sidestrand, which is very much smaller than its neighbour. The church of St. Michael, with round tower, was pulled down and rebuilt farther inland in 1880; this part of the coast is subject to severe erosion and several churches at different places have been washed into the sea, hence the moving of St. Michael's. In the east wall of the nave is a cross that could be Anglo-Saxon. Here again there is a good beach.

Priory Ruins

Five miles farther south is the larger village of Mundesley, with several hotels, a fine and extensive beach and a most pleasant atmosphere. The rebuilt church of All Saints contains a Jacobean pulpit and one Norman window. Four miles south of Mundesley is the coastal village of Bacton, which was considerably more

King's Lynn　　　　St. Nicholas Chapel—South Porch

Holkham Hall — Staircase, Middle Hall

HAPPISBURGH

important in past centuries for a little south of the village are the ruins of twelfth-century Bromholm Priory; the ruins are well worth viewing and entrance is made through an early Norman gateway; this is on private land and a request to view should be made at the farm. The church of St. Andrew has a thatched chancel and inside is a particularly beautiful piscina. There are several thatched cottages and houses, a good beach, with a concrete wall and promenade. The nearby Ostend Holiday Village has the usual array of chalets and beach huts, with ice-cream parlours, etc., serving the two old villages of Bacton and Walcott. There is an immense beach with rolling sand-dunes.

Happisburgh

The village of Happisburgh lies between the church and the red-and-white lighthouse. At the beach there is another small hamlet. The coast has been heavily protected by timber ramparts, over which steps give access to the very fine beach. The dominating church tower on the little hill is the most outstanding feature; it is close to the sea, well above it and 110 feet in height. Note the font and the piscina; the date of the original building was probably the fourteenth century. The lighthouse was built in 1791 to warn ships of the dangerous sands offshore.

Tower Windmills

Two miles south of Happisburgh and a mile from the coast is the village of Lessingham, where there is a small church with a prominent tower; the chancel is in ruins and the nave is thatched. It probably dates from the early fourteenth century. Sea Palling, the next coastal village, is a nondescript place of new building with a very few nice old cottages. A long line of sandhills forms the sea wall over which is a fine sandy beach so common along this coast. One mile to the west is a partly ruined tower windmill. Only one more village is passed before Horsey Mere is reached at the northern end of the Norfolk Broads; this is Waxham, with a partially ruined church that still dominates the village and one of the largest thatched barns in Norfolk. One mile to the south-west is the ruin of a further tower windmill.

Continuing southwards, the coast road passes right through the National Trust property of Horsey, which includes the Mere and a very fine preserved, white-painted, tower windmill. The church of All Saints is thatched and has a round tower that may be Norman or late Saxon. A little south of Horsey Mere is the coastal village of Winterton-on-Sea, with a jungle of sand-dunes and a great beach of mixed shingle and sand. The village is quite small, but a modern hotel with beach huts, many of them white-painted with thatched roofs, adds a touch of the tropical as well as a seasonal increase in population. Several more unimportant little places occur before Caister-on-Sea, which is about eight miles south of Horsey Mere, and Great Yarmouth, which is a further three miles.

GREAT YARMOUTH

Population: 52,970
Early Closing Day: Thursday
Market Day: Wednesday/Saturday
Tourist Information: (R) 14 Regent Street,
(R) Marine Parade (summer only)

GREAT YARMOUTH AND GORLESTON-ON-SEA are administratively one town and, since only a golf course separates Great Yarmouth from Caister-on-Sea, it is as well to deal with all three towns as one.

History begins with Great Yarmouth, which in the tenth and

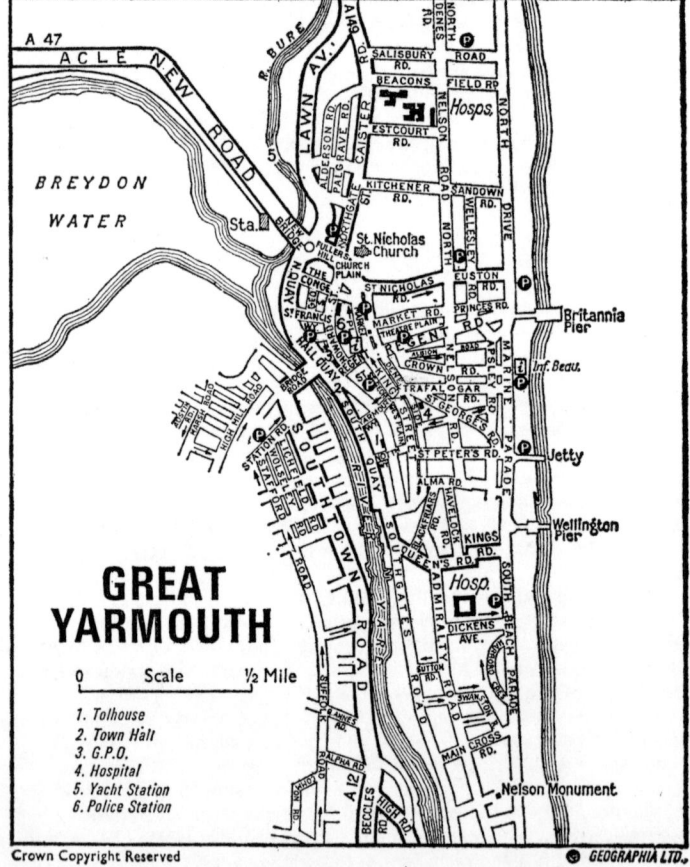

1. *Tolhouse*
2. *Town Hall*
3. *G.P.O.*
4. *Hospital*
5. *Yacht Station*
6. *Police Station*

GREAT YARMOUTH

eleventh centuries was a sandbank washed up by the sea and at that time peopled by a few fishermen. This sandbank caused the River Yare to change its course to the south, where it finally joined the sea about four miles south of its original outlet. By the time of the first charter, when Yarmouth became 'Great', in 1208, this sandbank was well above the waves and was peopled by fishermen and merchants; for a harbour had grown along the east bank of the River Yare and Yarmouth was well on the way to fame as a mercantile and a herring port. Today the importance of the mercantile port is greater than ever, but the fishing industry has gone; after the First World War it fought a losing battle and nothing remains of the great herring fleets that, within living memory, sailed from Yarmouth.

Old Yarmouth

The town occupies a narrow strip of land between the Yare, Breydon Water and the sea, but of late years has extended northwards. Old Yarmouth was a walled town with its face towards the river and walled off from the sea. Some lengths of this wall, which was begun in the thirteenth and completed in the fourteenth century, can still be viewed. Mariners Road, Blackfriars Road, St. Peter's Place and Town Wall Road are probably the best places.

The Rows

The principal streets of the old town ran from north to south but were joined to each other and to the Quayside by a large number of Rows, very narrow passageways some of which were no more than two feet six inches wide; there are said to have been over 100 of these. During the Second World War, bombing destroyed most of them, but a few remain. In these Rows lived not only sailors and fishermen but rich merchants; a few of their houses can be seen today. The Quayside is undoubtedly the most important remnant of medieval Yarmouth and it is said to be the finest quay in Britain. One pointer to the importance of medieval Yarmouth is the fact that there were four priories, the Franciscans, the Dominicans, the Carmelites and the Benedictines, all contributing to the religious life of the town.

Restored Church

The Elizabethan Museum is a Jacobean house with a Georgian front. It has been furnished to illustrate life in the sixteenth and seventeenth centuries; it is in the South Quay and is the property of the National Trust.

The parish church of St. Nicholas stands four-square beside Church Plain and behind it are the Priory Gardens with the refectory of the original Priory, dissolved in the sixteenth century. In front of the refectory is the Vicarage, a charming eighteenth-century building of mellow, rosy brick. Much of the original church of St. Nicholas was destroyed during an air-raid in 1942, but it has been impressively restored in the Gothic manner. It is still held to be the largest such parish church in England. Also in Church Plain stands 'Fishermen's Hospital', a delightful group of almshouses. In the middle range of buildings, under a cupola, stands a statue of St. Peter, patron saint of all fishermen.

Close by is Sewell House, of 1646, the birthplace of Anna Sewell, the author of *Black Beauty*.

Ancient Inns

In King Street the White Lion, of Elizabethan origin, should be seen, as well as several Georgian houses. Along the quayside Hall Quay has two very old inns: the Duke's Head, dated 1609, and the Elizabethan Star Hotel. South Quay shows a sequence of fine old houses dating from 1596 to the eighteenth century; among these and standing a little back from the pavement is the old Merchants House, of seventeenth-century brick with a slightly later front; this and another similar house in Row 111 have been restored by the Dept. of Environment and opened to the public as museums. A little off South Quay is the Tolhouse, of 1362, which was badly damaged during the war but has been well restored; it contains dungeons and a display illustrating local history and is open to the public. Near the Tolhouse are the remains of the Greyfriars Priory of the thirteenth century.

The Promenade

Nineteenth-century Yarmouth, some of the newer shops, hotels, the sea front and all that goes to make a modern seaside holiday resort, is built between the position of the one-time town walls and the sea. The Promenade extends from the North Denes (which, although once an area of sand-dunes has been converted into a racecourse, a caravan camp and a golf course) to the South Denes, a distance of about four miles. At the south end there is another very large caravan camp and camping site. A little inland from the Promenade stands the monument to Lord Nelson. Along the whole length of the promenade are the attractions which include a funfair, swimming pool, winter gardens, the round Marina Theatre, restaurants, cafés and just about everything the fun-loving holiday-maker could ask for.

Gorleston

Gorleston-on-Sea, which is connected to Yarmouth by ferry across the Yare but can only be reached by road over the bridge two and a half miles away, is in fact a resort in its own right; it developed with Yarmouth in the nineteenth century but is a very much quieter place. An extensive beach of sand and gravel backed by the grassy cliffs, a swimming pool and pavilion, greens and walks along the cliff-top and a quiet and tidy town make a very attractive, though not excessively ornamental, resort. The parish church, St. Andrew's, was originally 14–15th century but the present fabric is mainly Victorian restoration. There are some very early brasses, but much mutilated. In the south aisle note the royal arms of George I.

Caister

Caister-on-Sea is essentially a busy place and a dormitory for Great Yarmouth. There is an immense beach, largely of fine sand, a caravan camp and a lifeboat of which the locals are rightly proud. Northwards are sand-dunes and some new housing estates, but there is plenty of room on the beach.

Sir John Falstaff

Two miles west of the town and just south of the west road, the A1064, is Caister Castle, which was built in 1432–35 for Sir John Fastolf. The remains, which are moated, are extremely impressive and include the ninety-foot tower with stair turret, gatehouse and some sections of the walls. A climb may be made to the top of the tower from where a fine view of the surrounding country may be had. Shakespeare's creation of 'Sir John Falstaff' is said to have been inspired by the character of Sir John Fastolf. There is a museum with a large collection of early motor cars, and the castle is open daily during the summer.

Roman Town

A little north of the town, beside the A149, are the remains of the Roman town which preceded the present Caister. It was built in the second century on the slightly higher land overlooking the open estuary and the sea. At that time a great deal of the low-lying land here was marsh, which has since been drained. Much excavating has been done and interesting conclusions drawn. The Dept. of the Environment have tidied up the site and part is preserved for public viewing, which includes a portion of the south gate with a nearby length of wall, and part of a large building that was probably a hostel for seamen. At the time of the Danish invasion, towards the end of the ninth century, this first town of Caister was deserted and the nucleus of the present town started.

Port and Docks

A word must be said of the port of Yarmouth and the rivers Yare and Bure. The port is known as the Gateway to the Broads and as such will appeal to the yachtsman. Industrially the port is important for sea-going ships and those that trade along inland waterways. Ships of 500 tons gross can steam up the River Bure to Norwich Power Station and those of 300 tons can steam to Norwich docks on the outskirts of that city. The River Bure will carry the yachtsman to the northern broads, while the Waveney, a tributary of the Yare, will carry him to the southern broads. Finally, Yarmouth, in conjunction with the docks, has a thriving industrial section, largely light.

Section 3   The Broads

THE NORFOLK BROADS ARE SET IN A TRIANGLE, the three points of which are Stalham in the north, Norwich to the west and Lowestoft at the south-east corner. They consist of a very large number of shallow lakes joined by six rivers, all of which, after much meandering, flow into the North Sea via Breydon Water and the River Yare at Gorleston. There are some 200 miles of navigable waterways extending from Yarmouth and Lowestoft to Hickling Broad near Stalham in the north, and right into the heart of that fine city of Norwich in the west.

    The navigation authority for the Broads is the Great Yarmouth Port and Haven Commissioners, 21 South Quay, Great Yarmouth. Every yachtsman or operator of a launch should have a copy of *Norfolk Broads and Rivers*, published by Blakes (Norfolk Broads Holidays) Ltd., in association with Geographia, and at least some knowledge of sailing and/or navigation. Some of the waters are privately owned, some are restricted as to certain uses, some, such as Horsey Mere with the white-painted windmill, are National Trust property and Bird Sanctuaries.

Facilities

    The Broads and the connecting rivers are well supplied with landing places and most hotels will give information free of charge. Boats, yachts and launches may be hired or visitors may use their

Norfolk Wherry

own craft. There are very numerous boatyards where service and supplies can be obtained. There are also a large number of hotels throughout Broadland, but it is necessary to book well in advance for the boating public increases every year.

Broadland Rivers

While most of the Broads are linked by meandering waterways, a few are isolated lakes. Many are hidden from the roads, but a sail or the upperworks of a launch will frequently be seen as if it is sailing over the land; this is because most of the waters have high banks and a different level from the roads. The six rivers of Broadland are the Yare, the Waveney, the Bure, the Thurne, the Chet and the Ant. The Waveney joins the Yare at the western end of Breydon Water, while the Bure joins at the eastern end, very close to Yarmouth. There are a number of excellent and informative books on the Broadland waters for the assistance of those who intend touring by water. Some knowledge is absolutely necessary.

Berney Arms Mill

The principal Broads are, in alphabetical order, Barton Broad, Hickling Broad, Horsey Mere, Hoveton Great Broad, Ormsby Broad, Oulton Broad (which is in Suffolk), Ranworth Broad, South Walsham Broad and Wroxham Broad. Most of these, and many others, will be found to have boating facilities at the waterside villages as well as hotels. The New Cut, an artificial waterway, joins the rivers Yare and Waveney. The northern end of the New Cut is at the village of Reedham, where the Berney Arms Mill should be seen; it is in the hands of the Dept. of Environment and is open to the public.

There are no towns within Broadland, but there are a number of villages, both large and small. Oulton is fast growing into a town, Wroxham and Hoveton together are very popular and developing fast. On the outskirts, Yarmouth and Lowestoft are on the coast and make a first-class stepping-off point for a holiday on the waters of the Broads. To the south, Beccles and Bungay are both on the River Waveney, by which the Broads can be reached.

Fish and Wildfowl

Some fine fishing can be had, most types of coarse fish, with the occasional trout and some gigantic pike, offer possibilities of an excellent catch. Licences may be obtained at most of the larger villages. Wildfowling can be undertaken in winter and the necessary information on this subject is obtainable from most of the waterside hotels. The Broads have an enviable reputation for both wildfowling and fishing and good sport is almost a certainty.

Prior to the end of the nineteenth century this tract of country was little known and satisfied purely local needs. One of these was the harvest of reeds which were, and still are to a lesser extent, used for thatching. Wildfowling and fishing were not sports in the modern sense but in fact a harvest of food on which the local population relied to a very considerable extent. Since the end of the nineteenth century the Broads have been discovered and utilised to an ever growing extent by the sailing and boating public from all over these islands until today tourism, with the special attractions of sailing and motor boating, has become virtually the only industry.

Somerleyton

A great deal of the Broads country is very beautiful indeed and many motorists, who do not venture on to the water, visit this piece of country. Nevertheless it remains a fact that only the water-borne holiday-maker can obtain anything like a useful knowledge of the Broads country or enjoy the many real pleasures that this comparatively small, but absolutely unique, area of East Anglia offers. There are several places of outstanding beauty that the motorist can easily visit. Somerleyton Hall and Gardens are open to the public at certain times; the Hall and the village are set in an outstandingly beautiful piece of countryside, the village is a gem, with its thatched cottages, wide open aspect and glorious trees; it is situated five miles north of Oulton in Suffolk.

Fritton Lake

Next door to Somerleyton is Herringfleet, a lovely village with an old church with round tower and thatched nave. Three miles farther north, on the A143, is St. Olave's Priory, built of flint and brick; it is under the care of the Dept. of Environment. Two miles nearer Yarmouth there is a side road signposted to Fritton Lake; here the Hall is a guest house while the gardens, the parklands and the lake are open to the public as is the fishing. The village church is thatched and has a round tower. Blundeston Church, five miles north of Lowestoft, has a round tower of A.D. 988. Loddon, on the A146 between Norwich and Beccles, boasts a fifteenth-century church with a two-storey porch and a Jacobean pulpit. Acle on the A47 has a church with an eleventh-century round tower and a font of 1410. St. Benet's Abbey lies off a side road between Ludham and Ranworth; it is a very beautiful ruin dating back to A.D. 816 and was one of the religious foundations endowed by King Canute. The Gatehouse remains: there is also a windmill.

Potter Heigham

The parish church of Potter Heigham dates back to about A.D. 1200 and contains much that is of very great interest: it is thatched and has a round tower. At Ranworth the church of St. Helen has a complete rood-loft and Norfolk's finest screen, which is painted with pictures of saints. These and many other villages offer the visitor their varying beauty of location, their churches, their cottages and old farmsteads and all that has gone to make the distinctive character of the Broads.

Section 4 The Norwich Area

NORWICH

Population: 120,096
Early Closing Day: Thursday
Market Days: Wednesday and Saturday
Tourist Information: (N) Augustine Steward House,
14, Tombland

THE LARGEST CITY, county town of Norfolk and big industrial complex, Norwich is a modern place yet with roots deep in the past. It is set comfortably in the midst of some of the finest agricultural land outside the Fens; it is almost in the centre of Norfolk and is still the agricultural focus of the area. In addition, it is a yachting centre and the hub of the cultural life of the county. It is provided with all the modern amenities as well as being the point from which both rail and roads radiate.

Wensum Loop

The modern city is considerably intermixed with the many remaining medieval parts of Norwich and this again adds to its charm. The Castle, the Cathedral and the River Wensum are the three chief points from which to start an exploration. The Castle stands guard on the highest of the many hills (not of great altitude but often steep) upon which Norwich is built. It is very much the city centre and almost all of the oldest and finest buildings are situated east and west of the Castle and within the wide north-easterly loop of the River Wensum. At the very heart of this loop is the great Cathedral with its green Precinct, neighbouring Bishop's Palace and colleges. Norwich is also a river port where boats of smaller tonnage still trade.

Famous Institutions

Stone Age and Bronze Age settlements have been found in the area, the Romans had a fort or small town not far away and of ourse the Saxons were here. It was the Normans who built the first castle, a wooden Motte and Bailey which was soon replaced by the stone Keep. During the following centuries to the present time it has been as a market and a trading centre that Norwich has really grown to its present position; as the hub of one million acres of rich agricultural land this was the natural and inevitable development.

Barclays Bank originated here, the Norwich Union Insurance Group was founded in 1797, and these two famous institutions serve to reflect the financial and trading past. The first notable manufacturing industries concerned the weaving of yarn from the Norfolk wool, for until the nineteenth century wool was the life blood of agriculture in what is now virtually an entirely arable country. In the sixteenth century a third of the population of Norwich were refugees from religion-torn Europe and it was the weavers who had fled from the Low Countries who introduced the craft to this area. Worstead, a village ten miles away, gave its name to the particular yarn known as 'worsted'.

Changing Industries

By the middle of the eighteenth century the water power and the early steam power developed in Lancashire and Yorkshire proved the undoing, and eventually the end, of the hand-looms of other counties. Today, new industries of diverse kinds have helped Norwich to grow to an important city with a charm that has something to do with the people, the broad East Anglian sky and the delightful mixture of old and new.

Ancient Buildings

An exploration of the more ancient buildings might well start with the Cathedral, the building of which began in 1094; by 1145 it was complete and Bishop Herbert de Losinga transferred the Bishopric from Thetford to Norwich. The replacement of the Norman roof took place in the fifteenth and sixteenth centuries, the upper parts of the choir and presbytery were rebuilt in the fourteenth and the spire was added in the fifteenth century. The remainder of the structure is virtually all original Norman.

Historic Gates

Norwich Cathedral was served by monks from the attached monastery. The Close, once part of the monastic grounds, adds considerably to the beauty of the view of the Cathedral while the cloisters remind us, more perhaps than the Cathedral, of the ancient past of the whole area. The cloisters are rare, if not unique, in having a floor right round and above the cloister court. There were four gateways to The Close; the Ethelbert Gate was rebuilt in 1316 in the Decorated style and is very ornate; the Erpingham Gate of 1420 is reputed to be one of the most beautiful gatehouses in England. These two gates give on to the upper Close, a rich green lawn surrounded by Georgian houses with some fine trees. The water-gate is lower down by the river at Pull's Ferry, a noted beauty spot named after an eighteenth-century ferryman. The gate itself is of flint and stone and was probably the most popular gate in the days of water travel. The Bishop Gate (no longer in existence) stood at the western end of Bishop Bridge.

The Cathedral

The walk up through The Close to the two top gates and the Cathedral is a fine and beautiful introduction to one of the greatest Norman cathedrals in the country. The exceptionally long nave, with its massive piers forming arcades, is almost overwhelming in its appearance of soaring height and grandeur. The roof is embossed with carvings depicting stories from the Bible which may be inspected either by looking through the mirror-tables there, or with the aid of binoculars if the visitor wishes to make a detailed study of the work. The original Bishop's Throne is of stone, the only other like it in England is at Hexham Abbey in Northumberland. The choir-stalls are notable for remarkable carving of the canopies and the misericords below the seats. Through the Nave Screen Arch lies the chancel or presbytery, which also impresses one with its great height, for it is considerably taller than the great nave.

Nurse Cavell

The grave of Nurse Edith Cavell is in 'Lifes Green', a tranquil spot on the south-east side of the Cathedral, and the pathway thence leads to the 'Great Hospital', or Almshouse, founded in 1249 by Walter de Suffeld who was then Bishop of Norwich. There are many other historic and interesting relics of medieval Norwich to be seen in the course of a stroll around the Cathedral grounds.

Tombland

Just above the upper Close is the broad tree-lined square known as Tombland, which derives from the Saxon word for market. This is a particularly pleasant place, giving on to the Erpingham and Ethelbert Gatehouses. Here is a statue to Nurse Cavell, the Maid's Head Hotel, apparently of no interest, but hiding behind its new front a seventeenth-century building on the site of the medieval Maid's Head Inn, the fifteenth-century church of St. George and Samson and Hercules House (a seventeenth-century house that takes its name from the two porch pillars). On the corner of Tombland Alley is Stewards House, half timbered and dating from the very early sixteenth century. This particular area contains two closes, the old grammar school, the Bishop's Palace and a number of houses of various periods.

Elm Hill

Elm Hill is a narrow, cobbled and medieval street, one of the most fascinating in the city. Here coffee may be taken in a thatched house that was the Britons Arms and probably of the fifteenth or sixteenth century. The north side of Elm Hill has been restored by the Corporation and includes the Strangers Club of Elizabethan vintage, the house of John Pettus who was Mayor in 1590, and the medieval church of St. Simon and St. Jude which is now a Boy Scouts' club. At the top of Elm Hill is the former church of St. Peter

Hungate, dating from 1460; it is now an Ecclesiastical Museum.

Close to the top of Elm Hill, but in St. Andrew's Street, is St. Andrew's Hall which, dating from the fifteenth century, is one of the finest examples of Perpendicular architecture in England. At one time it was the nave of the church of the Black Friars and is now used as a civic hall; the chancel of the same church is now known as Blackfriar's Hall. Opposite St. Andrew's is Suckling House, a fifteenth-century City Merchants' banqueting hall. Nearby is St. Andrew's Church, which was rebuilt in the very early sixteenth century and contains a memorial tablet to Abraham Lincoln. Facing St. Andrew's Church is the fourteenth-century house of William Appleyard, first Mayor of Norwich, which is now a museum of Local Industries and Crafts; it is known as the Bridewell.

Riverside

Along or close to the riverside are several places that should not be missed: note, for example, the remains of the fourteenth-century City Wall, with two Boom Towers, lower down on the river. A little farther south is King Street, and Music House, which is the oldest house in Norwich and possibly the oldest in the United Kingdom; it was erected in the eleven-hundreds. Also in King Street are the houses of several medieval families. Farther north, at the bottom of Bishopgate, is the Bishop's Bridge of the thirteenth century and one of the oldest in the country. Close by is the Great Hospital, which was founded in 1249. At the Reformation the chancel of St. Helen's Church was converted to a hospital; note the magnificent roof of 1385. A little farther west along the river is the fourteenth-century gateway to the Bishop's Palace, while opposite is the house of John Sell Cotman the painter.

Sir Thomas Browne

Among the very many places of interest and beauty not so far mentioned, that should be seen, are the Strangers Hall of the fourteenth century; St. Peter Mancroft Church of the fifteenth century, where lie the remains of Sir Thomas Browne, the philosophic physician whose beautiful, measured prose in such works as *Urn Burial* and *Religio Medici* make them world classics; the Guildhall of the very early fifteenth century in the Market Place; and the Maddermarket Theatre, a replica of an Elizabethan Theatre where plays and other performances are held. This by no means exhausts the list of historic and interesting places which Norwich has to show the visitor.

The Castle

The age-old centre of Norwich is the Castle on its hilltop where a fascinating museum will be of paramount interest to most visitors. For something like 900 years the great square Keep of Norwich Castle has stood guard over the city. The first Motte and Bailey was

NORWICH

constructed in 1067 and the stone castle was built in the early eleven-hundreds. In 1220 it became the County Gaol and remained so until 1887 when the City bought the Castle for conversion to a museum and public park. Among the many features of interest are the old spiral stairway to the dungeons, professional sculpture-work and the rude carvings of prisoners, the fighting gallery and the chapel, the twelfth-century entrance to the Keep with finely ornamented doorway and realistic carvings.

Old and New

A small booklet can be bought in the Castle which gives an abbreviated history of one of the oldest castles in England. Acting as complete contrast to this fine old Norman stronghold the new University of East Anglia is situated at Earlham, only two miles from the city centre.

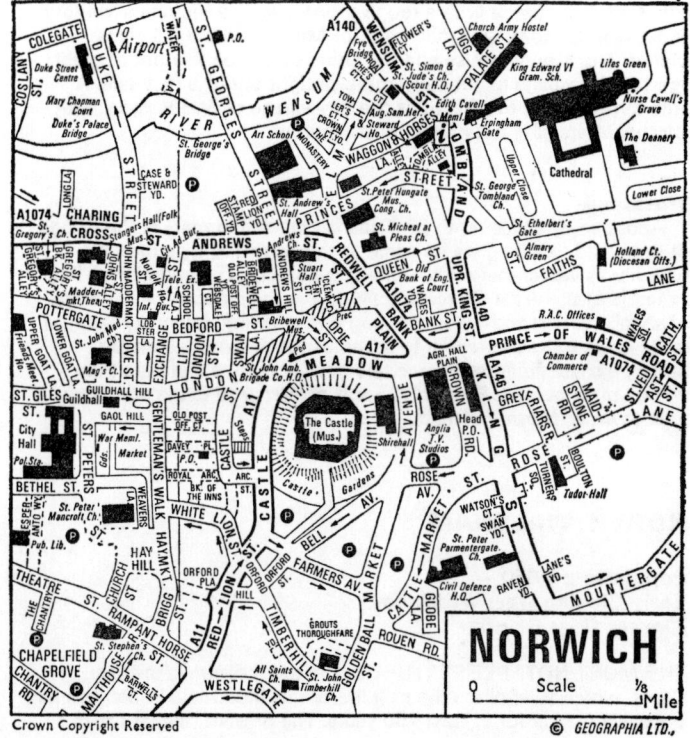

NORWICH TO NORTH WALSHAM, BLICKLING HALL, AND AYLSHAM

EAST OF NORWICH the A146, the A47 and the B1140 will carry the motorist through the Broads country to the coast. The A1151 heads north-east through rich agricultural land, well broken by spinneys and woods, along the north-western edge of the Broads to Hoveton, Stalham and the coastal road. A minor road, the B1150, heads north through several tiny villages to Coltishall, a distinctly Georgian village with a thatched church. Pleasure boats can reach Coltishall from the Broads along the River Bure. At nearby Buxton there is a watermill that was operating until 1912; at that time barges traded between Buxton and Lowestoft but now only small boats can reach Coltishall. The R.A.F. have a station in the vicinity.

A side road which runs very close to the River Bure will take the motorist to Maylon Bridge where there is an Elizabethan Manor House and, nearby, several fine thatched barns. At Great Hautbois, on the Bure and very close to Maylon Bridge, is a quite remarkable little thatched church with a rough round tower, a Victorian window and a Norman font. One mile north of Maylon Bridge is Lamas Manor. The Manor House and the church are probably not of great age but the village might have come straight out of a fairy tale. A little farther along the B1150 is the tiny village of Sco Ruston, with another interesting but partly ruined church.

Worstead

About seven miles north of Coltishall, on a side road, is the village of Worstead, which gave its name to the particular type of cloth which was woven here in the fifteenth century. The church is a fine example of the wool churches built during the prosperous centuries of sheep-rearing and wool-spinning and weaving, generally thought to have been the fourteenth to seventeenth. A thatched manor house, a small green and some fine trees complete a picture that will be remembered. Four miles north of Worstead is the attractive little town of North Walsham.

NORTH WALSHAM

Population: 6,650
Early Closing Day: Wednesday
Market Day: Thursday

THE MOST NOTABLE FEATURE of the town centre is the Market Cross, which symbolises the past life of this little town which has had a weekly market for at least 700 years. The present Market Cross

NORTH WALSHAM

dates from the fire of 1600 which destroyed most of the town; on view inside the Cross is one of the earliest fire engines.

North Walsham was one of the prosperous wool markets and the church of St. Nicholas, which was built in the fourteenth century, is another example of the wool churches. During the intervening centuries a part of the tower collapsed. Close to the Norwich road there is a Cross commemorating the Battle of North Walsham Heath, which took place in 1381 during the Peasants' Revolt. Close to the Yarmouth road is the last windmill in this area; it is one of the now very rare post mills; these were the earliest of all the known windmills.

Fisher's Theatre

One member of the old Paston family, famous for the Paston letters, founded the Paston School which, after 360 years, is still a flourishing source of education for the district. Lord Nelson was one of its more distinguished pupils. North Walsham has been the scene of much cultural activity; the present Church Rooms were Fisher's Theatre; the Fisher family had a number of theatres in Norfolk and performed comic operas and straight plays by many authors. North Walsham attracted a certain amount of notoriety on account of the smuggling for which this little town appears to have acted as a clearing house. During the seventeenth and eighteenth centuries cock fighting, steeplechasing, at least one great prize fight and Fisher's Theatre attracted great crowds and brought both fame and business to the town.

In 1825 the Dilham or North Walsham Canal was built, connecting North Walsham with the waterways of the Broads; this proved of considerable value until, in 1874, the railway was extended to the

Blickling Hall

town and the canal slowly declined and finally died. Today, pleasure boats can get as far as Dilham.

Unspoiled Countryside

The countryside for many miles around North Walsham is well wooded, very gently undulating and completely unspoiled. Agriculturally it is today good productive land and falls between what may be termed the lighter barley lands of the north and the stiffer wheat land of the south. Although sheep brought prosperity to North Walsham and maintained it for nearly 500 years, there are today virtually no sheep in Norfolk; cattle followed the sheep in Norfolk's history, yarded cattle treading the muck that grew the barley and the wheat; now there are very few yarded cattle and only a few dairy herds. Ninety per cent of Norfolk's one million or so acres is under the plough and to some extent artificial fertilisers have replaced 'old-fashioned muck'.

A little more than three miles north of the town is the village of Trunch, where the Perpendicular church of St. Botolph has a magnificent font canopy, one of only three of this type in England; a fine hammerbeam roof adorned with angels and a painted early sixteenth-century screen. In this area there are many tiny picturesque villages and much rustic scenery well worthy of a little exploration.

Felbrigg Hall

Three miles south-east from Cromer and signposted off the A148 to Holt and Fakenham is the fine National Trust property of Felbrigg Hall, a very fine seventeenth-century house in contrasting styles, set between the Great Wood and a fine sweeping park. Rooms of the highest quality, and pictures largely of the eighteenth century, including a complete collection made on the Grand Tour are on show. There is an Orangery with remarkable camellias, and a walled garden lately restored to its former glory, with flowers, fruit trees, vines, herbs and vegetables. The Woodland Walk gives access to Felbrigg Woods, still the haunt of the red squirrel.

The Barninghams

A little farther west, by some delightful country lanes, will be found the three Barninghams. North Barningham has a partially restored thirteenth-century church of St. Peter; unlike most Norfolk churches, St. Peter's is a small one, but contains much of interest. North Barningham Hall was built during the first few years of the seventeenth century and is largely in ruins, although still of interest.

Little Barningham, or Barningham Parva, has a church which, much restored, boasts a Jacobean pew on which stands the figure of a skeleton with a scythe and hour-glass and the inscription 'As you are now even so was I, remember death for ye must dye'.

Barningham Town, or Barningham Winter, is not of great interest apart from Barningham Hall, which belonged to the Paston family

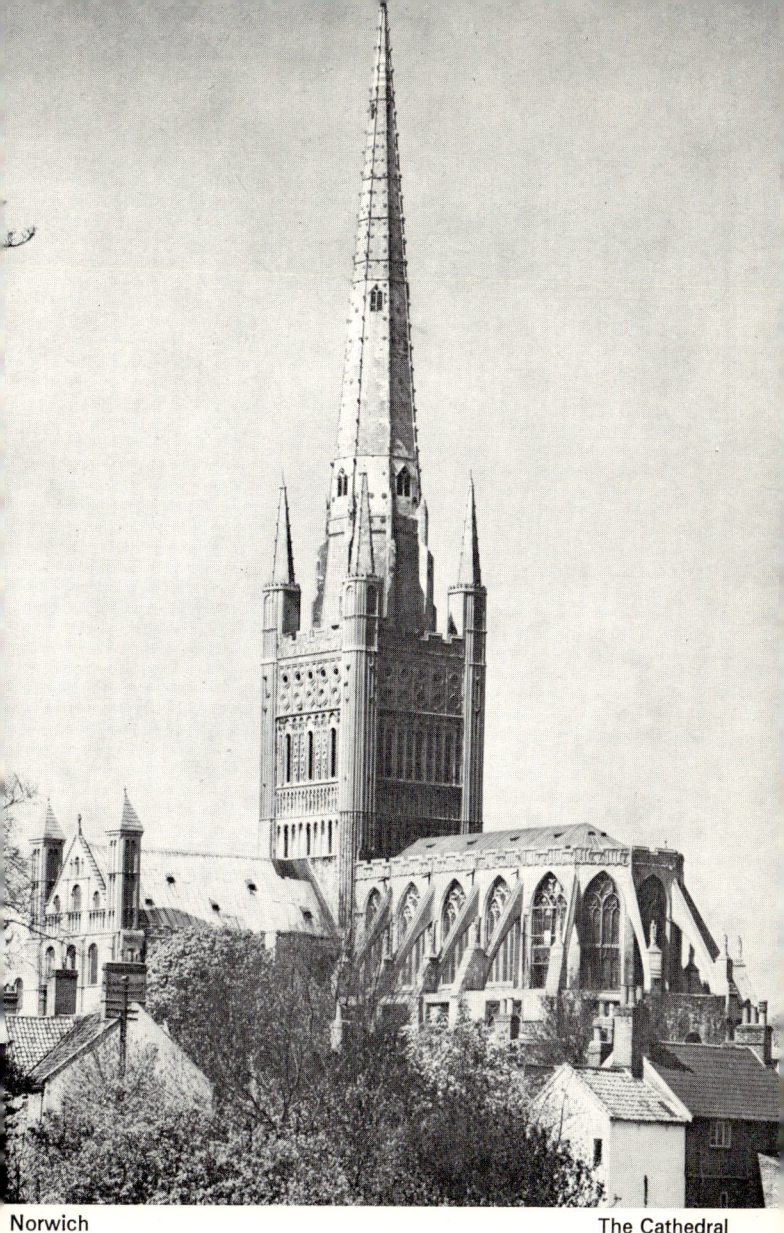

Norwich — The Cathedral

Earsham — At the Otter Sanctuary

Castle-Acre — Typical Norfolk Town Sign

AYLSHAM

and was built in 1612. A great deal of the seventeenth century remains, although parts were rebuilt in the first few years of the nineteenth century.

In the same area is Baconsthorpe Castle, in the hands of the Department of the Environment and open to the public. Sometimes referred to as Baconsthorpe Hall, this was neither the one nor the other, but a well-fortified manor house built by the Bacon family in the latter half of the fifteenth century; a great deal remains that is of absorbing interest.

Great Show-place

Blickling Hall, two miles north of Aylsham and a little west of the A140, is one of the show-places of East Anglia. It is in the hands of the National Trust and on certain days is open to the public. The Hall was built in 1616–24 and is a magnificent example of the Jacobean style in red brick. The first sight of Blickling from the main road is calculated to make us stop and wonder whether we are living in the twentieth century or the sixteenth. The outside of the house, the gardens which contain many magnificent trees including some rarities, the lake, the orangery and the chapel are all on the same splendid pattern, with such a delicate and refined appearance that one finds it impossible to leave without a full exploration. The rooms, decorations and furniture, though rather more ornate, come into much the same category. As an example of craftsmanship some 350 years ago, this is an exceptional example of skill combined with exquisite beauty.

AYLSHAM

Population: 4,250
Early Closing Day: Wednesday
Market Day: Monday

AYLSHAM, ON THE A140 AND SOME TWELVE MILES north of Norwich, is a pleasant little town with a church that, although considerably rebuilt, originated in the fifteenth century. It is a wool church with much of the outside faced with knapped flint in the East Anglian style. Aylsham has a number of attractive houses dating from the early seventeenth century. On the way down the A140 to Norwich a stop might be made at the village of Marsham to see the remarkable timber-work in the roof of All Saints Church. The next village, Hevingham, boasts a church that was originally thirteenth century, an early wool church, while Horsham St. Faith, only four miles from Norwich, has the remains of the priory of St. Faith where now stands the derelict Abbey Farm; there are considerable Norman remains both in the house and the garden. The priory was founded in 1105. The Mission Room has a Norman arch from the priory. In the village there are some nice seventeenth-century houses.

NORWICH TO WALSINGHAM, FAKENHAM, AND EAST DEREHAM

THE B1149 RUNS IN A NEARLY STRAIGHT LINE over the twenty-two miles from Norwich to Holt, through country that is well broken with woods and is not generally too crowded; a very pleasant run. Over the first fifteen miles there is nothing of particular note, but where the road crosses the East Dereham–Aylsham road, near the tiny hamlet of Cawston, is the Duelling Stone in the care of the National Trust. Here, in 1698, Sir Henry Hobart of Blickling Hall was killed in a duel. In the hamlet of Cawston the Church of St. Agnes is well worth a visit. It is a wool church of 1414 with a chancel older than that at Hingham: here the hammerbeam roof is worthy of note, as is the piscina in the south transept.

Reepham

If the motorist continues west from Cawston, three miles will bring him into the village of Reepham, where long ago there were three churches in one churchyard; today two are left of which the parish church is St. Mary's of the thirteenth century with several good brasses and monuments. St. Michael's is Perpendicular, while the two vestries are linked together. Only a wall of the third remains. Reepham has a very pleasant Market Place with some nice old houses, some being half-timbered.

Norfolk Wildlife Park

From Reepham a country lane will take the visitor north-west to the equally tiny village of Guestwick where, in a field by the church, there is a Congregational Chapel of 1652. The church of St. Peter is of particular interest because it dates from the period—the late eleventh century—when Saxon architecture was giving way to the Norman. Four miles south of Reepham is the Norfolk Wildlife Park, founded by Philip Wayre in 1961. The first of its kind in Europe, it now has the largest collection of British and European birds and mammals in Britain, most on view to the public.

Salle Church

About two miles north of Reepham, superbly placed on the highest ground in the district, is the magnificent church of SS Peter and Paul, one of the most splendid fifteenth-century parish churches of England. The tower, containing eight bells, is 111 feet high. It has a fine nave, with slender columns rising to a lofty clerestory, a splendid seven-sacrament font, a magnificently carved roof, handsome brasses, fine misericords, a fifteenth-century painted wine-glass pulpit and a good Rood screen. This church, which is bigger than many cathedrals, is undoubtedly worth a visit.

LITTLE WALSINGHAM

Bullfer Grove

Four miles from Holt on the Fakenham road are two National Trust properties. The very small village of Bale stands a quarter of a mile north of the main road; beside the church, which is thirteenth century, there is a fine group of ilex trees where prior to 1860 there stood a mighty oak known as the Bale Oak; this measured thirty-six feet in circumference and was reckoned to be a thousand years old; it was removed in 1860. Almost opposite the Bale Oak and a mile or so south of the main road is a piece of completely wild forest land known as Bullfer Grove which will bring great pleasure to the lover of nature.

Binham Priory

Some six miles west of Holt, again by country lanes, is the thirteenth-century priory of St. Mary at Binham. Only the west end of the Priory Church survives and this is used as the parish church. Considerable remains of other parts of the church can be viewed, but unfortunately there is not much left of the monastic buildings. There is, however, sufficient to give an idea of the original layout. Binham Priory is in the hands of the Dept. of Environment and is open to the public.

Little Walsingham

A quiet country lane will take the motorist in less than five miles to Warham, where there are two old and interesting churches. Five miles south of Warham is Little Walsingham, the scene of pilgrimage from the twelfth to the sixteenth century. The village itself is outstanding and completely unspoiled, a nice mixture of Tudor and Georgian with some half-timbered houses dotted about on the hillside and obviously all built before the days of town planning. The main road and the Market Place are perhaps the best parts of an extremely attractive village.

The church of St. Mary was extensively damaged by fire and the inside has therefore been rebuilt, and rebuilt very well indeed. In the churchyard are some magnificent Scotch firs which add greatly to the scene. The ruins of the Augustinian Priory, including the gateway of 1440, and the grounds, are open to the public at certain times when one may take a very pleasant stroll in delightful surroundings. Just outside the village on the Fakenham road are the ruins of the Greyfriars Friary of the fourteenth century, they are part of a private residence but are open to the public upon occasion. Although there is nothing remaining that is complete, the ruins are of great interest.

The ancient pilgrimage was to the Shrine of Our Lady of Walsingham, set up within the priory. It was very much a feature of the religious life of England in the Middle Ages and well into the sixteenth century, for it was a more practical pilgrimage for most people than the difficult journey to Compostella in Spain (Shrine of St. James), Rome or Jerusalem. In the 'Percy Reliques' there is an anonymous ballad testifying to the fame of Walsingham. It begins:

> 'As ye came from the Holy Land
> Of blessed Walsingham,
> O met ye not my true love,
> As by the way ye came?'

Indeed, Shakespeare could rely upon his audiences recognising and understanding Ophelia's quotation from it when, in her mad scene in *Hamlet*, she sings:

> 'How should I your true love know
>   From another one?
> O, by his cockle hat and staff,
>   And his sandal shoon!'

An Anglican pilgrimage was revived in the nineteenth century, centred upon a new shrine set up in a building with a tall, brick-built campanile, in Little Walsingham village. Since 1921 the Roman Catholic pilgrimage revival has centred upon the Slipper Chapel at Houghton St. Giles, some two miles south of Little Walsingham.

Showground Organs

Six miles from Little Walsingham, on the Fakenham–Holt road, stands the village of Thursford. Here, at Laurel Farm, is a famous collection of showground organs, many of them from fifty to a hundred years old, and one may spend an entertaining time among them.

A little over three miles south of Little Walsingham, on the Fakenham road, is one of the most outstanding manor houses in East Anglia, built in the late fifteenth and early sixteenth centuries. It is of red brick in true Tudor style, with twisted brick chimneys, great buttresses and a porch bearing the Royal Arms worked in brick. The best view of East Barsham Manor is from a hilltop to the south.

A turning to the right out of East Barsham leads on to the B1355, where a further right turn at six miles brings one within sight of the ruins of Creake Abbey, which is under the Dept. of Environment protection though open to the public.

The church of St. Mary at North Creake should be visited for a sight of the fine hammerbeam roof, while the church of St. Mary at South Creake should be seen for the hammerbeam roof, the roodscreen and other ornaments.

Houghton Hall

Some six miles south-west of South Creake is the Palladian mansion of Houghton Hall, built for Sir Robert Walpole in the eighteenth century. Its magnificent state rooms, furnishings, art collection and china are open to the public on certain days. The house, the home of the Marquess of Cholmondeley, is set in glorious parkland.

FAKENHAM

Population: 4,500
Early Closing Day: Wednesday
Market Day: Thursday

SETTLED SNUGLY ON THE NORTH BANK of the River Wensum, Fakenham enjoys a position of importance as the market town for this part of the rich Wensum Valley. Market day is Thursday. It has Saxon origins and a busy and dignified appearance. The church of St. Peter and St. Paul, which has a tall fifteenth-century tower, dominates the town from its hilltop position. It is largely of the Decorated and Perpendicular periods with an Early English doorway. The Crown Hotel may well be the oldest house, it was certainly a posting house in the coaching era and stands alongside what was probably a Roman road from Newmarket to the north coast near Burnham. It is a good shopping town and an excellent stop. Three miles south-west of Fakenham, and still in the Wensum Valley, is Raynham Hall, which was built in 1630 for a member of the Townshend family. Although this house is not open to the public it can be seen from the church, for both are in Raynham Park; South Raynham has a delightful little church with an eleventh-century altar.

Wensum Valley

Along the A1067 to Norwich there is not a lot of interest beyond some pleasant villages and some grand scenery, for most of the journey is along the Wensum Valley—rich, verdant and well wooded Where the main road crosses the B1110, turn right for three miles to the village of North Elmham, where the ruins of an early eleventh-century Saxon cathedral are close beside the ruins of a manor house of 1386; both are within a moated enclosure. These buildings have probably not been much altered since the date of erection.

The Lincoln Family

Norwich is twenty-two miles south-east of Fakenham, while the nicest road to East Dereham is the B1146, which passes through Brisley where, in the fourteenth-century church, some original murals have been uncovered; this road, in a very pleasant thirteen miles, takes the motorist into East Dereham. However, by turning left just before entering East Dereham, or in the town itself, Swanton Morley may be visited. The ancestors of Abraham Lincoln originated here and the remains of their house are now incorporated in the Angel Inn which, with four acres of land, is owned by the National Trust. Samuel Lincoln, who emigrated to America in 1637, moved to the nearby town of Hingham for a few years before leaving for America. The church is another fine wool church and contains much of interest, including a plaque of the Lincoln Seal in the Perpendicular east window.

EAST DEREHAM

Population: 9,700
Early Closing Day: Wednesday
Market Day: Tuesday/Friday

ALTHOUGH EAST DEREHAM IS TODAY a manufacturing town it still has a good deal of the atmosphere of its one-time agricultural importance. The Georgian houses, which have, in many cases, been fitted with modern shop fronts, retain for the town centre that dignified air that makes an otherwise busy place a restful and pleasants spot in which to shop.

'Bloody Bonner'

Among the many items of interest to the visitor the most attractive is probably the small group of cottages known as Bishop Bonner's Cottages; they are just outside the church in St. Withburga Lane; they date from 1502 and are thatched. Bishop Bonner was Rector in 1534–40. The cottages contain a museum of local interest.

Bonner was later created Bishop of London by Henry VIII, imprisoned in the Tower during the reign of Edward VI, but released on the accession of Mary Tudor. During her reign he presided, by virtue of his office, over the Councils which examined the Protestant 'heretics' and condemned to the stake those who remained steadfast in the new faith. Because of this Bonner earned the soubriquet of 'Bloody Bonner', but it is fair to say that he was one of the first of Mary's clergy to sicken of these cruel persecutions.

St. Withburga's Well

The parish church of St. Nicholas was originally Norman but has work of every period to the Perpendicular. There is a lantern tower at the crossing and a detached bell tower built in the sixteenth century. Apart from Norwich Cathedral, and possibly St. Margaret's Church, King's Lynn, St. Nicholas is considered the most notable church in Norfolk. Inside there is a wealth of most interesting ornaments. In the churchyard is St. Withburga's Well, over which the inscription reads 'Younger daughter Withburga of Annas King of Angles died A.D. 655'.

Assembly Rooms

The Vicarage was built in 1807 but still retains the moat of the medieval vicarage which it replaced. The Assembly Rooms of 1756 are perhaps the most distinguished of the town buildings. Above the High Street entrance to the Market Place is one of the very fine town signs for which Norfolk is rightly famous; it represents the foundation of the parish by St. Withburga thirteen hundred years ago. East Dereham is a well-equipped little town with an unusually pleasant atmosphere.

EAST DEREHAM

Poor Box

Six miles south-west of East Dereham, on the B1110 at the village of Shipdham, is a church with a thirteenth-century tower topped by a small cupola and spire which contrasts with the battlemented tower; some parts of the church are Norman. Six miles beyond Shipdham is Watton, a small town where there is a Norman church with round tower; unfortunately the building has been considerably altered by the Victorians who, however, have left the Poor Box with its grinning figure and the inscription 'REMEMBER THE POORE 1639' written across his chest. In the High Street there is a clock tower dated 1679, with the local lock-up in the base; it was built after a fire in 1673 that almost destroyed the town. The tower held a bell that was intended to warn the inhabitants should another fire break out. Watton is on the extreme edge of Breckland.

Link with New England

The pleasant little town of Hingham lies seven miles east of Watton on the Norwich road. There are many fine examples of Georgian houses here. The great flint-built church is another example of the wool churches and is certainly worth a visit. Hingham in Massachusetts was founded by a group of emigrants in the early seventeenth century from this little town, which also numbers amongst its more notable citizens an ancestor of President Lincoln. Some fourteen miles of delightful country not far from the River Yare, to which the road draws closer as it travels eastwards, separates Hingham from Norwich.

Bishop Bonner's Cottages

NORWICH TO WYMONDHAM, DISS AND BUNGAY

THE ROAD FROM NORWICH TO WYMONDHAM, a distance of nine miles, is pleasant without being spectacular in any way. Wymondham is, in some ways, little short of spectacular; it is one of the most interesting towns in Norfolk, with a wealth of fine old buildings mixed with the modern shops so that the medieval town plan has survived.

WYMONDHAM

Population: 9,500
Early Closing Day: Wednesday
Market Day: Friday

FOR MOST VISITORS the first sight of old Wymondham will be the Market Place and Market Cross which was erected in 1618 on the site of one destroyed by fire in 1615; this one had served the town for 350 years, about the same age as the present Cross. On closer examination the ancient woodwork will be found to carry carvings of many of the articles that were produced by the woodworking industry of the town, an industry that made the place famous throughout the Middle Ages.

Abbey Church

The Abbey Church is, of course, the pride of Wymondham. It was founded in 1107 and building was completed, with one tower, in the late thirteenth century. During the early years continual disputes erupted between the monks and the townspeople largely over which part of the church each should use. In 1249 the dispute was referred to the Pope and a settlement was agreed upon which lasted but a short while. In consequence the crossing tower was destroyed and east and west towers built. There is an excellent little booklet sold in the Abbey which tells in some detail its history.

Historic Buildings

Probably the oldest house in Wymondham is the Green Dragon Inn, which is thought to date from the late fourteenth century and displays some magnificent timber both inside and outside; in addition there are some fine carvings and many features that are extremely rare.

Among the oldest buildings is the chapel of Thomas à Becket which was founded in 1175; not a great deal of the original building remains, most of what we see today is of the Decorated period to the late fifteenth century. Since the Dissolution of the Monasteries this

WYMONDHAM

fine old chapel has had a varied and somewhat extraordinary career. It has been a grammar school, a coal-house, a lock-up, the fire engine garage and a hall for entertainment; in 1888 it became again part of the Grammar School and is now a branch of the County Library.

Manor House

The old Manor House in Bridewell Street is another half-timbered house of great age which may have been an inn at one stage in its long life. On a beam over the doorway has been inscribed the following in Latin: 'MY SERVANT IS NOT A DORMOUSE NOR IS THY HOST A LEECH'. In one of the downstairs rooms is the following inscription on another beam: 'RICHARDUS LYNCOLNE, ANNODOMINNI 1616—LIVE WELL AND DIE NEVER, DIE WELL AND LIVE EVER'.

Period Charm

A couple of hours of quiet exploration will reveal many of the beauties that are rarely seen in this age of speed. In Market Street there are many early seventeenth-century shops that have, in some cases, had new fronts fitted. Damgate Street is another example of the past, where many of the houses were built against the priory wall. Close to Damgate Bridge across the Tiffy is the Sun Inn, although now a private residence, but with the Inn sign still flying; the Sun was a hostelry for several centuries and probably dates from the late fourteenth or early fifteenth century.

'Rush Murders'

In the area immediately surrounding Wymondham there are a number of very fine Halls and Manor Houses; most are of the seventeenth and eighteenth centuries but all are extremely fine examples of period building. These are Wattlefield Hall, Gunville Hall, Burfield Hall, Browick Hall and Cavick House, which is in the care of the National Trust and can be seen by appointment. Stanfield Hall is a genuine Tudor house and was the scene of the 'Rush Murders' in 1848, when the Recorder of Norwich, Isaac Jermy, and his son, were murdered by James Rush. All of these are private residences. Four miles north-east of Wymondham and a little south of the Norwich road is Ketteringham Hall, one of the most graceful Tudor houses in the vicinity and built in 1537. It is occupied by a car manufacturing company who use it as a training centre.

Ketteringham Manor dates from Saxon times and the church of St. Peter contains slight Saxon remains and much from the Norman period, as well as some interesting brasses and other monuments. Opposite the church is a small medieval house of the late fourteenth century.

Seven miles south-west of Wymondham is the valley of the Thet; in its upper reaches is the small market town of Attleborough which, apart from the church of St. Mary, has little of interest. The church is, however, a great attraction on account of the truly magnificent choir screen which, dating from 1500, extends right across the nave and both aisles. It is a beautifully carved creation and contains among its intricate workmanship twenty-four shields with the arms of the episcopal sees of England at that time.

Motor-racing Circuit

About seven miles west of Attleborough, on the very edge of the heathland of West Norfolk, is the multi-gabled and intensely picturesque Elizabethan Breckles Hall, which was built in 1583 and somewhat altered in 1901 and 1908. Outwardly its appearance is much as it was when it was constructed. Still on the verge of Breckland, and six miles south-west of Attleborough, occurs the village of Snetterton, with an interesting church dating from the twelfth or thirteenth century and the motor-racing track constructed from an ex-R.A.F. airfield which runs alongside the main road.

Unusual Interest

Old and New Buckenham are two villages of unusual interest. They lie a little to the north of the B1077, some six miles south of Attleborough. Old Buckenham is distinguished by its immense village green with several ponds, the whole surrounded with cottages. North-east of the village is the site of a castle and Augustinian priory, virtually nothing remains except the square moat which surrounded the castle. New Buckenham came into being in 1150, when a castle was built here to replace the ruined one at Old Buckenham; a circular moat encloses what remains, which consists of the round keep and an outbuilding that was the castle chapel, with some arches and a doorway. New Buckenham village is built tightly around the Market Place and the Market House of the sixteen-hundreds, with the wooden whipping-post, which has survived the centuries. The church is far grander than the village leads one to expect and contains a fine hammerbeam roof to the nave.

Banham Zoo

Three miles south is Banham Zoo and Woolly Monkey Sanctuary. Open daily all the year, the zoo specialises in the rarer primates, and 1975 saw the birth of both a Silver Leaf Langur and a Saki.

At the zoo there is also an International Motor Museum with cars which include Rolls-Royce, Alfa Romeo, Healey, Jaguar, Mercedes and Lancia. Motorcycles are featured and there is a Vehicle Adventure Playground.

To the south-west, and drawing near to Breckland, is the small town of Kenninghall, with a square of pleasant Georgian houses and a church of Norman origin with the arms of Elizabeth I over the altar of a small chapel. These are a very rare survival and occur in a place where Mary Tudor stayed but, so far as known, Elizabeth did not.

Immediately south of this corner of Norfolk is the River Waveney and the boundary with Suffolk. Although there is not the immense variation in scenery over the East Anglian countryside which may be found in many parts of Britain, nevertheless there is a continuous and, perhaps, more subtle variation which is the essence of East Anglia's attraction. The Valley of the Waveney is very beautiful without being spectacular in any way; the A1066 will take the motorist as far as Diss where the A143 continues the eastward journey to the Broads and the sea.

Bressingham Hall

Close to the source of the Waveney is the village of Bressingham, where the church of St. John the Baptist has some interesting features, including the arms of Charles II over the tower arch. Bressingham Hall is famous for its gardens, which have one of the largest collections of hardy perennials and alpine plants in England. An unusual attraction is the miniature railway which runs round the grounds, and also a remarkable exhibition of early steam-engines from 1890 onwards. The gardens and exhibition are open to the public on Thursday and Sunday afternoons during the summer.

DISS

Population: 4,230
Early Closing Day: Tuesday
Market Day: Friday

IN SPITE OF ITS CLIPPED AND UNROMANTIC NAME the little market town of Diss retains many of its old houses and shops and virtually the whole of the medieval street plan. It is a fascinating little place built around three sides of the Mere, a sheet of placid water of almost six acres, beside the very large village green. Around these three sides the town has carefully turned its back on the Mere while retaining it as a park and playground.

Market Place

The centre of the town is the Market Place, halfway up the hill on which the town is built; it is a busy yet very friendly little place. Among the older and more interesting buildings are the following: the Greyhound Inn, dating from the fifteenth century; Tudor House, with two magnificent king-posts, which is probably fourteenth century; the King's Head Inn of the coaching days; and the Dolphin, which is now a shop and café, but was an inn, and dates from the early sixteenth century. The Market Place and Mere Street are particularly rich in Georgian and eighteenth-century shops with unspoiled fronts. At the lower end of Mere Street, at the Mere itself, is the town sign, which reinforces the claim to friendliness.

Parish Church

Between the King's Head and the Saracens Head is the fine thirteenth-century parish church of St. Mary the Virgin, which is flint-built in the traditional style. In 1857 alterations and some rebuilding took place and now the chancel is regarded as one of the best examples of knapped flintwork in Norfolk. The west window of the South Chapel contains all the surviving pieces of stained glass from the original medieval window. Also to be noted are the ancient piscina and the Commandments Board, the latter at least 300 years old.

Roman Road

Three miles to the east is the A140 trunk road that the Romans first constructed 2,000 years ago; it has been a trunk road ever since. At the junction of the A140 and the A143, a spot that has been an important cross-roads for many centuries, there is one of the finest coaching inns in Great Britain. It was built of red brick in 1655 and resembles a mansion rather than a hostelry but, as the White Hart, still bids a welcome to the traveller as it did in the coaching days.

Pulham Market

Close by is the extremely nice village of Pulham Market which has grown around the church and the cross-roads with thatched cottages and a village green. One of the best Perpendicular churches in Norfolk may be seen at Shelton, some five miles north of Pulham Market by the leafy country lanes; a much earlier church was rebuilt in the early fifteenth century, while the tower is of flint, the body of the church is of brick; the interior is particularly handsome.

About eight miles from Norwich another fine Perpendicular church can be seen, at Saxlingham Nethergate. Here, the quantity of fourteenth- and fifteenth-century stained glass is remarkable, while the south window contains thirteenth-century glass, among the oldest in East Anglia.

The East Waveney

Eastwards along the Waveney Valley the river broadens and more and more pleasure boats will be seen. At Billingford there is a tower windmill on the immense green. This can be inspected by calling for the key at Mill House or one of the few cottages nearby. At Needham, the next little village along the riverside, the parish church is well worth a visit for within this simple building there is workmanship representing every period from the tower, which is early Norman, to some portions which are of the eighteenth century. Among the fascinating little oddments are some fifteenth-century bench-ends, a centuries-old chest, a Bible box with seventeenth-century decorations, and the huge lock on the tower door.

At Harleston, a little farther along the valley, one sees a small town that. although not very well known, is a wonderfully pleasant place with good Georgian houses, more especially in the Old Market Place.

The Otter Trust

Earsham, two miles from Bungay, is where the Otter Trust has been set up. Its aims are mainly to promote the conservation of these delightful creatures whose grace and intelligence together with their playful ways captivate all who have a chance to observe them.

Mr. Philip Wayre, Director of the Trust, has made available a thirty-five acre site by the River Waveney, and the venture is already flourishing. In encouraging breeding and conserving, the aim is eventually to release the young animals in suitable reserves to help build up the otherwise disappearing species. The Reserve is open daily, March to November.

BUNGAY

Population: 4,000
Early Closing Day: Wednesday
Market Day: Thursday

ALTHOUGH THE SMALL MARKET TOWN of Bungay is in Suffolk, because the A143 runs through the centre of the town it is convenient to mention it at this point. The great fire which almost destroyed the town in 1688 had the effect of making Bungay a Georgian or later town, with an agricultural and slightly industrial atmosphere. The Square is the centre of the town and, in the Square, the Butter Cross, erected in 1689, is the symbolic centre. The Town Reeve here takes the place of the Mayor in other towns; this title has existed since the earliest Anglo-Saxon days; he is elected by the Feoffees, a body established to regulate the town marshes.

Castle Gatehouse

The oldest building is the gatehouse of the eleventh-century castle which at that time included the present town site. The parish church of St. Mary is imposing in both its position and structure, it appears to be fourteenth and fifteenth century with later alterations. The church of Holy Trinity has one of the oldest towers in England, a round Norman one crowned with a later Perpendicular-style battlement; the chancel is thirteenth century and the pulpit Elizabethan with some fine carving.

The remains of the Castle and surrounding land have been acquired by the town council and converted into a park which is entered through a pair of very fine, modern, wrought-iron gates on which are depicted the Bigod lions; the Bigod family were the builders of the Castle.

Outney Common

On the outskirts of Bungay the National Trust have acquired nearly 500 acres of common land where the public have right of access on foot; this is a fine area of semi-heathland, over which there are grazing rights and a golf course. It is named Outney Common.

Close by at the village of Ditchingham there are fine old halls and a fifteenth-century church. A Roman brickfield with a kiln was discovered at Hedenham, three miles to the north, also four Roman burial urns which are now in the Norwich museum. An ancient tithe barn has been converted into a parish room while the Mermaid Inn in the main Norwich road is over 200 years old.

Ellingham village, on the main road to Great Yarmouth and two miles from Bungay, has a fine old mill and a disused lock on a small waterway, for this is the edge of the Broads. It also has an 800-year-old church which is of the greatest interest.

Brooke

Seven miles south of Norwich, a little east of the A144, at the village of Brooke, another church with a Norman 'round tower' can be seen. Several buildings in Brooke have been made the subject of preservation orders and it is a pretty place and unusual in that the main street divides round several meres or ponds. Despite its nearness to the county town, Norwich, Brooke has retained its distinctive identity and sense of community, winning several times recently the coveted title of 'Best Kept Village in Norfolk'.

Cornhall, Diss

Section 5　　　　　Breckland

THIS IS A LAND OF HEATH AND FOREST with a little heather here and there; a land of wide open skies with far horizons, a land where comparatively few people live; where the terrain is gravelly and sandy, where the rainfall is low, and for these reasons man has never cultivated the soil. And so today we are left with an area in which the walker and the car-owning holiday-maker can enjoy the out-of-doors with few restrictions. One word of warning: do not light fires near forests or rank top growth, during warm weather fires will spread uncontrollably and cause immense damage.

SWAFFHAM

Population: 4,300
Early Closing Day: Thursday
Market Day: Saturday

THE LITTLE MARKET TOWN OF SWAFFHAM is at the north-east corner of Breckland. From it radiate five main roads to the five towns of East Dereham, Fakenham, King's Lynn, Downham Market and Newmarket. It is a cheerful, smiling place of red brick with a particularly nice town sign which shows the Swaffham Pedlar. The market place is a wide junction of the five roads with no particular shape and the Market Cross, which was once known as the Butter Cross; this is built in the Palladian style and topped with a figure of the goddess Ceres holding a sheaf of corn. Around, there are some nice Georgian and Queen Anne houses.

Outstanding Church

The parish church is the most outstanding building and dates from the fifteenth century, although the outside is less than ornate the inside is a splendid example of the work of the period; the nave has a superb double hammerbeam roof. The chancel is the oldest part of the church and was built in 1454, the spire was added in 1510.

Peddar's Way

Castle Acre, which is some four miles north of Swaffham, is a pleasant, wide-streeted village with some slight remains of the castle but much more of the priory. It is on the line of the Peddar's Way, a road far more ancient than the Roman roads, that can be followed for some miles by walkers. The entrance arch of the castle spans Bailey Street and is flanked by towers, which are again flanked by shops; this is in the hands of the Dept. of Environment, as are the ruins of the priory, which should not be missed for they are among the best to be seen of their age, dating from the eleventh to the eighteenth century. The Prior's Lodging was occupied until comparatively recently. A very short distance from the priory is a Saxon church, at Newton by Castleacre; this is a far more interesting building than many a larger, better known church.

West Acre

Close by at West Acre, after crossing two fords over the River Nar, one comes to the remains of an Augustinian Priory of 1100 on both banks of the Nar; the fourteenth-century gatehouse remains, with some further ruins of the church and chapter house.

Seven miles from Swaffham on the King's Lynn road at Narborough there is an attractive church and Narborough Hall, which is partly Tudor. There are two fine watermills in the village.

Oxburgh Hall

The run to Downham Market can be made by very pleasant lanes which pass the National Trust property at Oxburgh Hall, which dates from 1482: the brick-built gatehouse is eighty feet high and may well be the biggest fifteenth-century gatehouse still in existence; the house is also brick-built and surrounded by a moat, while the gardens alone are worth a long visit. This is one of the finest halls in Norfolk and, being open to the public, should not be missed.

DOWNHAM MARKET

Population: 4,000
Early Closing Day: Wednesday
Market Day: Friday/Saturday

DOWNHAM MARKET IS A PROSPEROUS MARKET TOWN on the very edge of the Fens; it overlooks the River Great Ouse on the west side, while eastwards the Fens and rich agricultural lands give way to the forest and heath of Breckland. Although it is a pleasant town and an excellent place to stop, it has very little to show the visitor. Lord Nelson went to school here, the Crown Inn is seventeenth century and a most attractive hostelry. There are a number of eighteenth- and nineteenth-century houses.

To the south of the town, at the village of Fordham, is a little known brick-built house of 1480–90, it has buttresses with pinnacles and a fine Tudor chimney stack.

Grimes Graves

If the motorist takes the A134 from Downham Market towards Thetford he will, after eighteen miles, pass on the right the entrance to Grimes Graves in the care of the Dept. of Environment. Here may be seen some of the most remarkable remains of the work of Stone Age man. At that time flint was the best cutting tool. Here in the Weeting Valley was discovered a deposit of first-class flints. In this valley there are hundreds of pits of which some have been excavated; they are among the most interesting remains of the past in East Anglia.

Weeting Castle

On the B1106, which is a little west of Grimes Graves, another Dept. of Environment property of great interest will be found: it is Weeting Castle, which today consists of a moated enclosure with the ruins of a two-storeyed building with a tower or gatehouse.

The last eight miles from Downham Market to Thetford pass through forest-land with wide heathland to the east. There are many square miles around here which will attract the walker or the motorist who wants to stretch his legs or picnic.

THETFORD

Population: 16,000
Early Closing Day: Wednesday
Market Day: Tuesday/Saturday
Tourist Information: (L) Ancient House Museum, White Hart Street

THE LITTLE MARKET TOWN of Thetford sits in the southern end of Breckland and is entirely surrounded by heathland and forest. It is rather more ancient than some Norfolk towns and in the early eleventh century had, for a brief period, the Cathedral of East Anglia.

A great many narrow streets centreing on the Market Place represent the medieval town; the impression today is of Georgian builders. There are a number of houses of interest. The Bell Hotel has served the traveller for 300 years, the King's House has a fine Georgian front while another, of equal age, is Bridge House by the River Thet. The Ancient House of medieval date contains a collection which illustrates the history of man in Breckland.

The extensive remains of Thetford Priory, which was founded in the twelfth century, are under the Dept. of Environment and open to the public; they are very well worth seeing as are the remains of Warren Lodge on the Brandon road some two miles north of Thetford.

Thetford Castle was demolished in 1173, most probably the castle was a wooden motte and bailey: the mound remains, and can be reached by a pleasant walk from Castle Street over Castle Meadow to Castle Lane and the Dolphin Inn, which has the date 1694 on the wall. There are several other monastic remains in Brandon Road, London Road, near Euston Road and near the railway station; in the early medieval times Thetford had twenty churches and a number of monasteries, it was a much more important centre than it is today. Tom Paine, author of *The Rights of Man*, was born in Thetford in 1737.

Kilverstone Wildlife Park

Here, one mile north-east of Thetford, off the A11 in the grounds of Kilverstone Hall, are forty acres specialising in Latin American animals and birds, among them jaguar, puma, otter, squirrel monkey, macaw, parrot and penguin. There are separate ponds for flamingo, American and European water fowl. Special attractions, besides the young animals bred in the Park are: the walled garden with extensive herbaceous borders, a deer park, a half-mile riverside walk along the Thet, a picnic area and a water garden. The Park is open throughout the year, daily.

Euston Hall

This eighteenth-century house, home of the Duke of Grafton, contains a famous collection of paintings. The pleasure grounds were laid out by John Evelyn and William Kent. It is open on Thursday afternoons during the summer months.

The village of Euston is one of the loveliest of Breckland villages, with thatched houses set among tall trees, while the church is a delightful example of eighteenth-century architecture.

Thetford Priory ruins

Section 6 East Suffolk Coast

LOWESTOFT

Population: 55,000
Early Closing Day: Thursday
Market Day: Friday/Saturday
Tourist Information: (N) Amenities Dept., The Esplanade 🛏
(L) Town Hall, High Street

THE OFFICIAL COUNTY GUIDE SAYS: 'Lowestoft is remarkable for the variety and number of its attractions'. This statement is very true, for Lowestoft occupies an enviable position on the sea coast with a fine harbour, on the very edge of the Broads and connected thereto by Lake Lothing. Additionally it is at the eastern extremity of England and has been called the 'Town of the Rising Sun'. The authorities have successfully made Lowestoft one of the most popular resorts in East Anglia.

Burgh Castle

Looking back through the centuries we find that the Romans were very near to Lowestoft, for at Burgh Castle, some four miles west of the town, on the banks of the Waveney, Roman remains have been found under the ruins of the Castle. This is open to the public and is controlled by the Dept of Environment. Of historic old buildings Lowestoft has virtually none.

Fishing Fleet

Fishing always has been, and to a great extent still is, the life-blood of the town. Although the fishing fleets are not so great as in years gone by, Lowestoft is still one of the great fishing ports. Unfortunately the popular fish sales on the open dock are largely a thing of the past, the freezing plants buy and handle the fish in bulk.

Sea Front

The town may be conveniently divided into two parts, south of the piers and the harbour, and north of them. Northwards, the town fans out into a large shopping and entertainments area with the high spots along the two fine parades above The Denes. Lowestoft is exceptionally well provided with parks and open spaces, as well as some very beautiful gardens. Most of these will be found in this northern section, together with the bulk of the cinemas, theatres and the many and varied amusement centres. South of the harbour the

Claremont Pier may be taken as the centre of activities, but not as the shopping centre. North and south of the Pier lie the Esplanade and bathing beaches, farther south are the Kirkley Cliffs and a caravan camp. In all, the sea front covers some three miles, all of which provides pleasure or amusement of varying kinds.

The Harbour

The harbour area will be of interest to the boating enthusiast, and here will be found the Royal Norfolk and Suffolk Yacht Club, as well as the fishing fleet. The harbour, the Broads and boats generally are Lowestoft's chief attraction which, to a very large extent, is accounted for by the nearness of Oulton Broad, some two miles distant. The Nicholas Everitt Park, with its open-air swimming pool, affords an excellent opportunity of watching the activities on Oulton Broad.

Sparrows Nest

South of Claremont Pier the beach is excellent, sandy and firm, while bathing is safe at all states of the tide—thus it is a good place for family holidays. The northern end of the town, especially the Esplanade, is the quietest and will attract the older visitors. Boat trips to the Broads are among the most popular pastimes. The Cottage Museum of the Lowestoft and East Suffolk Marine Society is at Sparrows Nest, halfway along the North Parade and sea wall, and covers the history of fishing in Lowestoft. There are models and paintings of the old sailing smacks and the early steam drifters, of every phase of the fishermen's life and work, and the Museum should prove of absorbing interest to the many yachtsmen and boatmen who visit Lowestoft.

The Catch

Industrially the town is expanding, largely through the introduction of light industry and the growth of the freezing and packing plants which handle the bulk of Lowestoft's still large landings of fish. Although the landings of herring have sadly declined, mackerel, halibut and many other types of fish are plentiful. In 1920 the Ministry of Agriculture and Fisheries set up a laboratory to study, on an international basis, the problems connected with large-scale sea fishing.

To the South

Journeying south from Lowestoft the little church on the cliff-top will be noticed as the distinguishing feature of Pakefield, which is now a suburb of Lowestoft. Kessingland, the next coastal village, stretches from the main road to the beach. Here, in an area of outstanding natural beauty is the Suffolk Wildlife and Country Park. It is open daily throughout the year, and during the summer months refreshments can be obtained. There are many fine picnic spots, and there is ample parking space, as well as a play area for children. Lion, tiger, puma are to be seen, and among the birds one will find parrots, macaws, owls and vultures.

Southwards, the road leaves the coast and heads for Southwold on the western edge of a heathy stretch of country with a few patches of forest. A narrow lane leads to Covehithe, close to a particularly lonely section of the coast; this is a tiny village with a seventeenth-century brick-built church within the ruins of a much larger one. Next door is a thatched house and barn. This is a delightful spot for those desiring to get right away from the seaside-resort type of holiday. Six miles by car, but only four by the sea-shore takes the traveller into the nicest place on the coast of Suffolk.

SOUTHWOLD

Population: 2,250
Early Closing Day: Wednesday
Market Day: Monday/Thursday
Tourist Information Bureau: (L) Town Hall, Market Place

SOUTHWOLD IS A COMBINATION OF MODERN AMENITIES and the old world, one of the nicest seaside resorts on the east coast, especially for those desiring to leave all the bustle and tear of modern life behind. It sits on a low hilltop above the River Blyth and Buss Creek, which together make Southwold very nearly an island. The old town is delightfully and haphazardly built, with seven small greens dotted about among the houses and shops. These greens are a result of the great fire of 1659, when a number of houses and virtually all the public buildings were destroyed; many were never replaced and the vacant places show in these charming patches of green. There is a common, consisting of 130 acres of open grassland, which was presented to the town in 1509. The beach is a mixture of shingle and sand, the bathing is safe, while beach bungalows, bathing huts and deck-chairs are available.

Gun Hill

The principal green of the seven is South Green, which leads to Gun Hill, an open space on the cliff-top containing the six cannon presented to the town for its defence in 1745. On the same cliff-top stands the prominent white lighthouse, and in many of the cottage gardens the figureheads of old wooden ships can be seen. Probably the oldest house is Sutherland House in High Street, with magnificent seventeenth-century plaster ceilings and oak from a much earlier period. Although Southwold is a small town it was incorporated a Borough in 1490 by King Henry VII. The seventeenth-century Dutch gabled cottage in Victoria Street opposite the church is The Southwold Museum, devoted to a general collection pertaining to the history of the district, the Battle of Sole Bay and The Southwold

Railway which ran to Halesworth until 1929. Behind the Museum is a small library of books of local interest, as well as a great many pictures.

Southwold Jack

The church of St. Edmund is generally thought to be one of the finest Perpendicular churches in England and certainly the finest in Suffolk. Note the fine tall tower, the flintwork, the porch and priest chamber, the fifteenth-century south doors, the really magnificent roof-timbers, the pre-Reformation screen, the fourteenth-century wooden chest, the carved and painted reredos and lectern and the fifteenth-century painted screens, also the lovely figure of Southwold Jack. This is a 'Jack-smite-the-clock' figure, dressed in a model suit of armour (period Wars of the Roses), who strikes the bell of the church clock with his battle-axe. There are many such clock 'Jacks' in the area but Southwold Jack is the most attractive because of the accurate detail and colouring of his armour.

Heronry

South-west of Southwold, along the River Blyth, there are small areas of marsh, but apart from these the country is largely heathland and forest. It is extremely beautiful in the spring and autumn, the birdlife is sometimes prolific and the heronry set in the woods alongside the River Blyth adds a lot to the natural interests of the immediate neighbourhood. This is a small section of country, but is ideal for walkers.

Walberswick

Walberswick is one mile south of Southwold by the row-boat ferry —cars must go by Blythburgh, a distance of nine miles. The walk to the ferry is a most pleasant one and continued to Blythburgh makes a most enjoyable half-day. At one time Walberswick was a port with over a dozen vessels trading with places as far away as Iceland; at that time the River Blyth entered the sea at Dunwich; the final silting up of the river put an end to the port. The present church is built within the ruins of an older one and in fact is constructed out of the south aisle. Walberswick is a charming old place, as yet unspoiled. The beach here is immense and looks as though it continues so for many miles to the south.

Roman Sitomagus

The road south continues through or along the western edge of the heathland, interspersed with forest. By turning left through a large area of forest, Dunwich is reached. This place was once an important port and Bishopric with hospital and a number of churches. Today these are all at the bottom of the still-encroaching sea. In Roman

DUNWICH HEATH

times it was called Sitomagus, while in the seventh century it was a Bishopric and the centre of the religious life of East Anglia. Today there is a tiny cliff-top village with the remains of a priory and in a small museum the seals and maces with other relics of the former Dunwich Corporation. The cliffs, the beach and the village are all worth a visit by those interested in history.

Bird Sanctuary

Dunwich Heath is National Trust property and consists of 214 acres of sandy cliffs and heathland with a mile of beach. There is also a small lake frequented by sea birds; a car park is provided at the entrance and the whole area will prove a delight to the naturalist or to the family. It is approached by a turning off the Westleton–Dunwich road half a mile from Dunwich village and includes the Minsmere Bird Sanctuary. The countryside from Walberswick to well south of Dunwich consists of heathland interspersed with patches of marsh and is well provided with footpaths.

Hermit's Chapel

Several small villages are passed along the edge of the heathland before Leiston is reached. This is a small town that commenced its industrial life in the early nineteenth century with the manufacture of agricultural implements. Before 1365 there was a large Monastic Priory in the marshland between Leiston and the Minsmere River. These ruins, now known as the Hermit's Chapel, are two miles from Leiston, but are somewhat difficult of access. In 1365 this site was abandoned and an Abbey built close to Leiston; for many years after the Dissolution, the new Abbey was a farm with tithe-barn, granary and Tudor farmhouse, the ruins of which were restored after the First World War and have become a Diocesan Conference Centre and Retreat. There is much of interest in the old buildings, which are in the care of the Dept. of Environment, and visitors are made welcome.

Sizewell

On the coast just north of the little village of Sizewell is the new nuclear power station; the site has been well landscaped and has not in any way minimised Sizewell's attractiveness. There is a good beach extending almost to Thorpeness to the south, safe bathing can be enjoyed and although not a resort it does offer most of the modern amenities.

Thorpeness

Thorpeness is a quiet and very pleasant little resort with good bathing, a lake for boating, excellent sea fishing and a first-class golf course. It is three miles north of Aldeburgh by the coast road, which runs along the sea edge. There is also an all-the-year-round, heated swimming pool.

ALDEBURGH

Population: 3,100
Early Closing Day: Wednesday

ALDEBURGH IS AN OLD RESORT AND FISHING TOWN, as its name ('Old Borough' to the Saxons) indicates. Certainly it was well known to the Romans, for coins minted during their rule in Britain have been washed up from the sea and substantial Roman remains, notably a large villa, have also been excavated in the neighbourhood. A ship-burial uncovered some four miles out of the town indicates the presence of Angles, or even the Vikings, who raided along those shores. In the massive records of Domesday Book the 'Manor of Aldbure' is carefully documented, proving that the Conqueror's surveyors found it a thriving place.

Smuggling

Aldeburgh's golden years, however, were undoubtedly, from a commercial viewpoint, in the sixteenth century. This was the period of the 'Borough's' great fame as a shipyard and when it became also one of the chief ports. While the local fishing fleet went as far afield as Iceland for their catches, the local herring and spratting fleets worked the nearer waters. The less official source of prosperity, of course, was smuggling, which flourished along that coast, and many of the old inns of the town must have many an adventurous story connected with those daring escapades when the wily locals pitted their wits against the Excise men! Of the three best known inns, one, called The Three Mariners, was washed into the sea, but the Cross Keys and the Mill Inn have survived.

Slaughden

The shipbuilding yards flourished to the south of the town at Slaughden, a hamlet long since submerged beneath the sea. This was brought about by the gradual silting up of the estuary waters and the relentless depredations of the waves. The loss of this industry brought considerable poverty to Aldeburgh, which accounts for the rather gloomy portrait of the place as described in the work of the noted local poet George Crabbe, who was born there in 1745. Fortunately, after the threat of danger during the Napoleonic Wars, Aldeburgh achieved fresh if slow-growing fame as a holiday resort and the people who came in search of rest and recreation became a new source of prosperity to the place.

Crag Path

The oldest parts of Aldeburgh are those which are centred around High Street and very close to the sea; the more modern parts rise inland above the Church Hill where there is the golf club and, beyond it, the heathland and a very beautiful countryside. Between the old

ALDEBURGH

town and the beach runs Crag Path, a pleasant and unpretentious promenade. Extensive sea defences have been constructed along the front, for over the whole of the coast of East Anglia the sea is gradually eating away the land.

The Moot Hall

Among the interesting buildings are: Alde House, the home of Elizabeth Garrett, who became the first woman doctor of medicine and, in 1908, became the first woman mayor and magistrate; the Moot Hall, of the sixteenth century, which in parts probably dates from considerably earlier—the lovely Tudor chimneys are comparatively modern. It is still used as the Council Chamber and one room, containing a wealth of old maps and documents, is open to the public. The Martello Tower at the south end of the town is the most northerly of the chain of towers built in the early nineteenth century against the possibility of a Napoleonic invasion.

Church Hill

The parish church, which is situated at the top of Church Hill, is a very fine example of the Perpendicular in church-building. The tower is fourteenth century while the rest is probably fifteenth and sixteenth century. The long south porch of 1539 is peculiar in having three entrances. Note the Norman font, the seventeenth-century pulpit and the several brasses.

Birdlife

Aldeburgh has a lifeboat in which the town takes a lot of pride. The Alde estuary is famous for its birdlife and one of the rarer birds which has reappeared of recent years is the avocet which, not long ago, was regarded as a lost species.

Hollesley Bay

South of Aldeburgh, for some twelve miles the River Alde flows within a very short distance of the sea, is joined by the Butley River and, becoming the River Ore, they join the sea at Hollesley Bay south-west of Orford Ness. On both sides of this waterway are marshes, and only one town, Orford. Inland, away from the marshes, are some extensive areas of forest. The coast itself, between Aldeburgh and Felixstowe, is a paradise for the naturalist and ornithologist, while the River Alde is extremely popular with the yachtsmen.

The Festival

The Maltings, delightfully situated by the riverside in the village of Snape, four miles west of Aldeburgh, is the music centre for the celebrated Aldeburgh Festival. The Festival, founded in 1948 by

Benjamin Britten, Peter Pears, Eric Crozier and Imogen Holst, has achieved world fame for its promotion of cultural interests. One of its specialities has been interest in the work of George Crabbe, the Aldeburgh-born poet, and Britten's opera *Peter Grimes* was inspired by, and the libretto taken from Crabbe's poem 'The Borough'. The opera house and concert hall at Snape were literally made from buildings originally used for barley malting and were much admired for the excellent acoustics. In 1969 a major setback was suffered when the concert hall was destroyed by fire on the opening night of that year's Festival. Now triumphantly restored. The Maltings is often the venue for other musical celebrations apart from the special Festival.

Tunstall Forest

South of Snape the road to Orford turns south-east around the head of the estuary of the Alde and travels for about six miles along the edge of Tunstall Forest, which is unfenced and probably about fifty years old. It contains several blocks of the old red-barked Scotch fir, more characteristic of Scotland than of East Anglia.

Boating Centre

Orford is a quiet and largely unspoiled village close to the estuary of the Alde and therefore a popular boating centre. Orford Castle, under the Dept. of Environment and open to the public, was built between 1165 and 1173 by Henry II and was of great military importance. Only the Keep survives, this was round inside and polygonal outside, with projecting turrets. The parish church of St. Bartholomew was originally of twelfth-century date but that part of the church in use today is fourteenth century; the ruined chancel still remains. The font and screens are worthy of a closer look while the ruined walls of the Austin Friary will be noticed.

Ferry

From Orford the road runs through Tunstall Forest and, swinging around the head of the Butley River, runs parallel with the coast through several small villages to the mouth of the River Deben. Here a ferry can be taken to Felixstoweferry and Felixstowe, but only for the walker—the motorist must go by Woodbridge, a distance of approximately twenty-two miles.

Martello Towers

The village of Bawdsey at the mouth of the Deben has a church with a twelfth-century tower and sits to the south of several Martello Towers similar to the one at Aldeburgh. Between the coast and Woodbridge along the north of the River Deben there are several patches of forest, a number of quiet rural villages and much varied birdlife.

FELIXSTOWE

Population: 19,430
Early Closing Day: Wednesday
Tourist Information : (R) 91 Undercliff Road West 🛏
(N) Caravan, No 2 Gate, The Docks, (summer)

ALTHOUGH FELIXSTOWE, AS THE HOLIDAY-MAKER SEES IT, is less than fifty years old it is in fact a quite ancient place. The Romans are said to have built a castle here which has long since been washed into the sea. Felix, the first Bishop of Dunwich, is supposed to have landed here and bestowed his name upon the little town. A priory was founded at the time of the Norman conquest. King Edward III may have resided here at Old Hall in the fourteenth century and 300 years later the Landguard Fort was built.

Drama Festivals

The railway arrived in 1877 and right away Felixstowe commenced to grow as a resort and today is among the best on the east coast. The cliff and sea-front gardens are some of the finest to be found anywhere. Children are especially catered for and the swimming is safe at all states of the tide on a beach of clean sand and small shingle. Every possible amenity and amusement is provided, while nature supplies rather more sunshine than is general in England. During the spring and autumn the Felixstowe Drama Festivals are held and there is a Summer Show during the main holiday season. Dancing and many other attractions are available and the promenade is traffic-free, a great attraction to families. Sports of every kind are well catered for and many competitions are staged.

The Port

There is a certain amount of industry at Felixstowe, while the port is of considerable importance and is considered a major port for the Continent with a growing roll-on/roll-off container service. Outside the town industry is forgotten, for the countryside is very beautiful and is little spoiled. Within a few short miles a great many interesting and picturesque places will be found. There is a passenger ferry across the mouth of the River Orwell to Harwich, while Ipswich is only eleven miles away.

Landguard Point

Of the older and more picturesque buildings found in so many towns and villages Felixstowe has virtually none; little if anything is left of the Landguard Fort on Landguard Point, that finger of land which protects the Rivers Stour and Orwell, as well as the port of Harwich, from the north-east gales. The coast north and south of the town will prove of interest to the nature-lover and the ornithologist.

Section 7 Inland Suffolk

IPSWICH

Population: 123,500
Market Days: Thursday/Friday
Tourist Information: (N) Town Hall, Princes Street 🛏

THERE ARE PARTS OF IPSWICH which carry one's mind back to the days of horse traffic to a greater degree, perhaps, than any other large town in East Anglia. This is so because much of the medieval street plan has been retained, along with so many buildings from past eras which, combined with a modern outlook and excellent shopping facilities, form the great attraction of the town.

Cultural Centre

Ipswich, county town of Suffolk, is a port with particularly strong links with the Continent; it is a manufacturing centre with age-old traditions and many brand new industries; it is the hub of a large and prosperous agricultural community and the centre of the cultural life of Suffolk and much of Essex.

In addition, the Bishop resides in Ipswich, although his Cathedral is at Bury St. Edmunds.

Norman Walls

The origin of Ipswich, its growth and present-day importance are due to its position at the head of the River Orwell, which is, in fact, the estuary of the River Gipping and a number of smaller streams. It is not known who were the first settlers, but the Saxons were certainly here. The Normans quickly realised its importance as a port and during this period the town walls were built, as well as a castle. In the twelfth century, during the reign of Henry II, the castle was demolished and a century later the walls were rebuilt.

Ancient House

There is a great wealth of old and, in many cases, very beautiful buildings in Ipswich. The most beautiful and fascinating, if not the most important, is The Ancient House in Butter Market, which is a truly magnificent example of a half-timbered sixteenth-century house of the kind built by townsmen of means. The two upper floors project, while the decorative carving of the windows, etc., is unusually fine. The second floor has five very beautifully decorated bay

IPSWICH

windows and above the main doorway are the arms of Charles II who, it is said, once took shelter there. Within, the décor is as charming and splendid as the outside.

Dickensian Inn

In Tavern Street is an inn known far and wide as the Great White Horse; here Charles Dickens stayed and described it in *Pickwick Papers*; the Pickwick Room with Dickensian furniture can be seen.

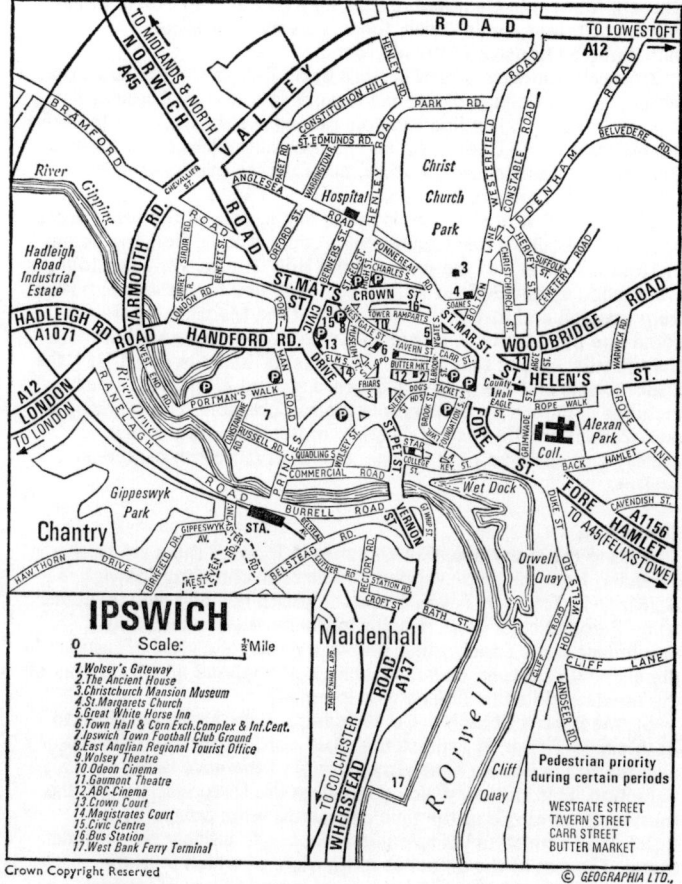

Today the Great White Horse is regarded as one of the great inns of England.

The situation of Ipswich on a main coach road into East Anglia naturally led to the establishment of a number of very fine coaching inns; among these may be mentioned the Crown and Anchor and the Old Neptune.

Tudor Houses

Among the many other buildings of note the following should be seen. A number of houses of the early seventeenth century in Grimwade Street close to the new Civic College; several Tudor houses in St. Nicholas Street and another near St. Mary Elms Church. Many fine Georgian houses may be found in Tower Street while, at St. Margaret's Green, there is a very handsome half-timbered house and the old Manor House.

Wolsey's Gateway, which is close to St. Peter's Church, is all that remains of the College of Secular Canons founded by Cardinal Wolsey in 1536. It is a fine example of medieval brickwork and above the archway is the Coat of Arms. The foundation stone of Wolsey's College is at Christchurch, Oxford, but a replica can be seen in Christchurch Mansion, Ipswich.

Christchurch Mansion stands in the public park of the same name and is a particularly fine example of a Tudor House. Building began in 1548 on the site of the priory of the Holy Trinity. Various additions were made up to 1735; in 1924 a half-timbered house was removed from Ipswich and re-erected as a wing of the Mansion. There are some fine period rooms, including a sixteenth-century kitchen with the utensils, etc., of that period, the servants' hall, the Great Hall, the Tudor rooms and many others. There is also an art gallery, which includes paintings by Gainsborough and Constable. The Mansion is an excellent and interesting museum of domestic furnishings, pottery and costume of the sixteenth and seventeenth centuries.

Churches

Among the many beautiful churches in Ipswich there are twelve surviving from the medieval period. The civic church of Ipswich is St. Mary-le-Tower in Tower Street; although recently reconstructed, some Perpendicular work remains in the nave. An interesting monument is the panel, which shows a panoramic view of Ipswich in the sixteenth century. There is much good knapped flint flushwork on the outside and some fine carving internally.

St. Margaret's Church in St. Margaret's Plain, and quite close to St. Mary-le-Tower, is perhaps the most worth-while from the visitor's viewpoint; the double hammerbeam roof of the nave being the chief attraction. This church, which dates from the Decorated period, the fourteenth century and the time of greatest wool prosperity for Ipswich, is a graceful yet splendid edifice with a finely proportioned tower. The rest of the churches of Ipswich, of which four are dedicated to St. Mary, each have some varied points of interest.

WOODBRIDGE

Population: 7,500
Early Closing Day: Wednesday
Market Day: Thursday

WOODBRIDGE RETAINS STILL THE ASPECT of a small seaport although it is thirty years since the last tramp steamer called. In the past there was a considerable amount of commercial shipbuilding; now only pleasure boats are launched from the stocks. Wool and the weaving of cloth, as well as other major industries (these included the manufacture of sailcloth and the malting of barley), did much to expand this little port and to enrich the townspeople.

Today Woodbridge offers endless opportunities for the holiday-maker, especially the yachtsman, for whom the twelve miles of the River Deben offers safe sailing in the most pleasant surroundings. The town is well supplied with riverside walks and parks and in the surrounding countryside there are many interesting places to visit. To the east, between town and sea, there is a large area of heath- and forest-land which is fine for picnic outings. On the sea coast there are marshes, shingle banks and some sandy beaches, and over all this countryside the birdlife is constant and plentiful with occasional rare visitors. In this area Rendlesham Forest will be a source of delight to all nature-lovers; it is sixty or more years old and contains many plantations of the red-barked Scotch fir.

Ricklinghall Inferior

Woodbridge School

In Woodbridge itself there are several old buildings that the visitor should not miss; the Shire Hall on Market Hill was built around 1570 by Thomas Seckford, the owner of Seckford Hall, which is now an hotel; this same Seckford was a judge under Queen Elizabeth and became the chief benefactor of the town; from his bequests has grown the Woodbridge School. The King's Head Inn on Market Hill is thought to be 500 years old while the Ancient House in Church Street dates from 1553. There are many nice Georgian houses and some half-timbered from the Tudor and Jacobean periods. The parish church of St. Mary has a tower which is visible for a great distance. Built of flint and stone, in the manner of the wool churches in the middle fifteenth century, and on the site of an earlier church, it is a good example of the period and contains much of interest. Outside the Bell Inn, itself probably Tudor, is an old lever weighing machine; it was used for the weighing of hay, wool and hides and is one of very few left in England.

Less than a mile south of Woodbridge, and right on the head of the Deben estuary, is an area of parkland named Kyson Hill and owned by the National Trust. From this beautiful and natural park some first-class views of the Deben and surrounding country can be had. Near the Ferry Quay the ancient tide-mill of the twelfth century can still be seen, while in Burkitt Road there is a preserved windmill.

All round Woodbridge, but particularly to the north, there are many villages, each with some point of interest or beauty; by the Deben River, by the River Butley and Rendlesham Forest, or in the richer agricultural land north and west of Woodbridge. Space allows the mention of but a few of these rural and unspoiled villages.

Historic Reminder

Butley, on the north-east edge of Rendlesham Forest, is one of the most historic spots in Suffolk, and, from some points of view, in England. Butley Priory was built in 1171 and the magnificent gatehouse remains; it was built by Ranulf de Glanville, who travelled with King Richard the Lionheart on his Crusades. Above this massive gateway are cut in stone the Arms of England and France, the Three Crowns of East Anglia, and heraldic devices of many other countries. Below these are the Arms or Heraldic Shields of many great East Anglian families. Around this historic reminder of times long gone is one of the oldest forests in Great Britain; Staverton Forest is said to have been here since pre-Druidic days and some of the oak trees certainly appear to be many hundreds of years old; it is a most fascinating place for any lover of nature.

Whipping-post

Halfway between Woodbridge and Wickham Market is the very lovely village of Ufford, with its companion Lower Ufford. Both are most picturesque, with half-timbered and thatched cottages, a few nice houses and a flint-built church 600 years old with one of the

Lowestoft Fishing port

Cavendish — Thatched cottages and St. Mary's Church

East Bergholt — Willy Lott's Cottage

finest font covers in the country. The ancient stocks and whipping-post still stand outside the church.

On the by-road between Wickham Market station and Pettistree there is a magnificent half-timbered house and watermill; they are in private hands, but a good view can be had from the gate. Wickham Market, which is two miles west of the railway station, is a very pleasant, unspoiled little town. To the north-west is Easton Farm Park, where past and present have been mingled to provide a fascinating glimpse of farm life through the years.

Sutton Hoo Treasure

Sutton village, by the River Deben, is famous for the excavation of the 'barrows', or burial mounds, in one of which was discovered a 'ship-burial'. The remains of a ninety-foot ship with a central cabin were uncovered and though the timbers had long rotted its impress in the clay was clear. The chemical compositon of the soil destroyed recognisable signs of a body, but judging from the wealth of gold, silver and enamel objects (some from far Byzantium and Alexandria) accompanying the burial, it was clearly a 'royal' memorial place raised like a cenotaph to honour the dead. It is thought now that it may well have been made for one of the Wuffinga dynasty, an East Anglian ruling family of the sixth to seventh centuries. The finds were presented to the nation by the owner of the land and are now in the British Museum.

Omar Khayyám

Some three miles north-west of Woodbridge is the village of Boulge, with a thirteenth-century church, and Boulge Hall, where lived Edward FitzGerald, the translator of the 'Rubáiyát' of Omar Khayyám; while at nearby Bredfield, where FitzGerald was born, the church, 600 years old, is well worth a visit to see the magnificent hammerbeam roof and the seventeenth-century oak pulpit.

Framlingham Castle

The market and agricultural town of Saxmundham is on the A12 six miles inland from the sea at Aldeburgh. It was an important coaching stop and today is largely modernised. The church is note-worthy for the very fine hammerbeam roof rediscovered in 1932. Seven miles west is Framlingham, an old market town of character. Framlingham Castle was built in 1190 by a member of the famous Bigod family in the period before square towers had been replaced by round ones. Although much inside the curtain walls has been destroyed, the walls themselves are intact with thirteen towers. There are few castles that have lasted the centuries as well as Framlingham, which is in the hands of the Dept. of Environment. In the town, Castle Street and Market Hill contain some good examples of domestic architecture; the seventeenth-century Ancient House and two sets of Almshouses of the late seventeenth century are notable

examples. The church of St. Michael is a rebuild of the original
fifteenth-century church; it is famous for the nave roof and
monuments to the Dukes of Norfolk and the Duke of Richmond.

Post Windmill
   At Saxsted Green, three miles west of Framlingham, is a very fine
post windmill under the care of the Dept. of Environment; this fine old
mill operated from 1700 until 1947; in all probability there has been a
mill on this site since the very early fourteenth century. At Dennington,
a short distance north, the church of St. Mary is of particular interest
for its sixteenth-century screens, its medieval stained glass and
seventeenth-century pulpit and box pews. At next door Badingham
the Norman church has a particularly fine tower and many interesting
ornaments, as well as an exceptionally fine nave roof.

Capability Brown
   Heveningham Hall, which lies between Laxfield and Halesworth,
was built in the late eighteenth century and the grounds were laid
out by Capability Brown. Much of the original furniture and most of
the original decorations remain; it is open to the public at certain
times. Close to the village of Yoxford there is an exceptionally fine
Jacobean house named Cockfield Hall; it was built in 1540 and part
of the original buildings are still occupied. It was here that Katherine
Grey, sister of Lady Jane Grey, lived out her last months.
   Farther north along the A12 is the village of Blythburgh, on the
River Blyth. At one time this was a small port and big fishing centre

Framlingham Castle

and a great deal larger than today. The White Hart Inn may revive some memories. The Southwold Railway once linked Southwold with Halesworth, but has vanished with the other great days of Blythburgh. The church of Holy Trinity is reputed to be the finest church in Suffolk; it is fifteenth century in origin, has been little rebuilt and is certainly a most handsome and imposing church.

Barnby

It is ten miles north from Blythburgh on the A145 to Beccles. The whole of this north-east corner of Suffolk is thickly dotted with picturesque villages, most have some feature of interest, all have their points of beauty in some degree, but all have the appearance of having grown with the trees and are an intrinsic part of the countryside, which varies from heath- and forest-land to rich arable land dotted with spinneys. Here one can wander about the countryside and find something new at every turning. One such find is at Barnby, where the little-known thatched church of the medieval period hides a Processional Cross cupboard door which is original and believed to be the only one in existence; next door at North Cove is a fifteenth-century church with Roman bricks in the tower and 600-year-old paintings on the Chancel walls; this one is also thatched.

BECCLES

Population: 8,300
Early Closing Day: Wednesday
Market Day: Friday

THE MARKET TOWN OF BECCLES is on the south bank of the River Waveney and right on the edge of the Norfolk Broads; this is its chief attraction and claim to fame. There are many more new buildings than old, a situation caused by a sequence of fires in the sixteenth and seventeenth centuries which all but destroyed the town. From the holiday-maker's viewpoint it is an ideal stopping place, a first-class centre from which to explore. For the yachtsman the River Waveney provides an excellent route to the Broads or the sea.

The buildings most worthy of note are several streets of Georgian houses, the old Town Hall of 1726, St. Peter's House, Ravensmere House of 1694 and Leman House of 1631. On the way to Bungay, Roos Hall, of 1583, should be seen. Apart from these, Beccles is a very pleasant but somewhat undistinguished place. Beccles Common, the Quay and Yacht Station are popular with holiday-makers. The parish church of St. Michael's is a fine and handsome edifice though not to be ranked with the best wool churches. The tower is sixteenth century, the rest fourteenth. The south porch is, possibly, the best of St. Michael's. The tower is detached from the body of the church because it was not considered safe to build such a massive tower so near the edge of the cliff on which the church was built; it is very close to the river.

Mettingham Castle

The country south-west of Beccles, between the River Waveney and the A1120, is a maze of country lanes thickly dotted with tiny villages. On the road to Bungay there is a very old round-towered church which stands alone; it is probably thirteenth century with a Norman doorway, excellent roof-timbers and a noteworthy font. Very near the above church is the village of Barsham, where the round tower of the church is Saxon. Farther along the Bungay road, at Mettingham, are the massive gateway and other ruins of Mettingham Castle, as well as a Norman church.

Smallest Borough

The municipal borough of Eye, which is some fifteen miles south-west of Bungay, is the smallest borough in the county, with a population of well under 2,000. The name is derived from the Saxon for an island; the small hill on which Eye is built was once surrounded by water. In Saxon and Norman times there was a castle and a little later a priory; today there are a few remains of the castle and the fish-ponds and Guest House of the priory can still be seen. The early sixteenth-century Guildhall is, perhaps, the best remaining building in Eye. The tower of the church is considered notable, being decorated with flint and stone panelling from the ground to the battlements.

Flemings Hall

Some six miles south-east of Eye is the tiny village of Bedingfield, where the National Trust have the very fine Tudor moated house known as Flemings Hall. Although this delightful old Manor is not open to the public it is possible to make application for an appointment. Farther west on the A143, in West Suffolk, and about fourteen miles from Diss one passes through Ricklinghall Inferior. The church here has a round tower topped by a fifteenth-century Belfry which has distinctive pinnacles. Next is the pottery village of Wattisfield, where bricks and earthenware have been made since pre-Roman days, while some six miles farther south, where the A143 crosses the A1088, is Ixworth Abbey, where an eighteenth-century house incorporates the crypt of the twelfth-century Abbey. Documents and manuscripts, as well as the ruins of the Priory Church, are on view.

Icklingham Church

North and west of Bury St. Edmunds and Ixworth the face of the countryside changes quickly as the Breckland and the border with Cambridge and Norfolk are approached; this is the country of heath and heather, of forest-land and wide spaces, where the walker will feel more at home. In this corner of Suffolk it is the countryside that is the chief attraction; however, there are one or two places worthy of note. A circular run from the attractive village of Ampton, around the outside of the estate, taking in Great Livermore, Ingham and Timworth, makes a delightful jaunt through natural woods for most of the journey. Euston Church, Thetford Heath (which extends over the border from Norfolk), the thirteenth-century church at Lakenheath where there is a large R.A.F. camp; these are all worthy of a visit, as are many more; but the finest little church in the whole of this area is the medieval church at Icklingham. Here, note the backless pews, the fourteenth-century chest and the thatched roof. This church is a great deal more fascinating than many a larger one.

Flint-knapping Centre

Mildenhall, which lies farther north towards the Cambridgeshire border, is a busy, modern town with a medieval Market Cross and a church of the thirteenth to fifteenth century with a magnificent hammerbeam roof; there are also some very fine Georgian houses. Brandon, fourteen miles north of Mildenhall and right on the border with Norfolk, is one of the major towns of Breckland and is the last remaining centre of the ancient art of flint-knapping.

Newmarket is in Suffolk but almost surrounded by Cambridgeshire. In this Guide it appears in Section 10, page 118.

This north-west corner of Suffolk, so very different from the rest of this verdant county that occupies such a prominent place in British agriculture, is full of interest and beauty; sparsely populated with miles and miles of heath and forest it is a land that can be enjoyed at all times of the year.

BURY ST. EDMUNDS

Population: 28,000
Early Closing Day: Thursday
Market Day: Wednesday/Saturday
Tourist Information: (N) Abbey Gardens, Angel Hill 🛏
                        (summer only)

BURY ST. EDMUNDS, the largest town in western Suffolk, is the only cathedral town in the county. Its motto, 'Shrine of a King, Cradle of the Law', sums up its history, its traditions and its outlook.

A Saxon settlement known as Beodricsworth already existed on the site of what was to become Bury St. Edmunds, when, in A.D. 630, Sigebert, King of the East Angles, endowed a monastery there. Towards the end of the eighth century King Offa of Mercia ruled East Anglia, and when his only son took to the religious life he was obliged to look elsewhere for a possible successor. He did not wish the new peace of his kingdom to be destroyed by faction at his death. During his travels in Europe, Offa met Prince Edmund at the court of his cousin Alkmund, King of Saxony. Struck by the youth's noble nature and Christian piety he chose him as his successor before proceeding on pilgrimage to the Holy Land. In 855, worn out by his travels, Offa died, assured that his choice for the succession was a sound one, and when the young Saxon landed at Hunstanton later that year crowds of his new subjects lined the way to see him. On Christmas Day, A.D. 856, Edmund was crowned, being then fifteen years old. He had studied his royal duties under Bishop Humbert of Elmham and for the next ten years strove to establish the rule of Christian law in his kingdom, setting a great example to his people by his own wise, orderly and virtuous life.

Treachery

The treachery of a banished offender, guilty of murder, brought the Danes down upon the shores of East Anglia. Berne, a hunter, set adrift at sea as a punishment for his crime, was washed up on the shores of Denmark. There he told the rulers that King Edmund had had their father Lothroc put to death, though it was this particular murder of which he himself had been guilty. The marauding Danes, primed by the treacherous Berne, landed in the north and, when spring came, descended upon East Anglia, burning, destroying and killing.

Christian Martyr

The saintly king, now twenty-five and in the heyday of young manhood, hoped that if he gave himself up to the marauders they would spare his people, and accordingly he and Bishop Humbert surrendered themselves to the enemy. Finding that they wished to force him to abjure his religion, Edmund refused. Thereupon he suffered the same martyrdom as St. Sebastian, for he was tied to a tree and then shot through and through with arrows. This occurred at Hoxne, where the brave king died protesting to the end his Christian faith. Most of his subjects had been hiding in the woods to save themselves from the fierce Danes and many of them witnessed the awful scene. Finally the enemy warriors struck off King Edmund's head and tossed it into the deep woodland. Then they killed the faithful Bishop Humbert.

Shrine

After some days, when the Danes had gone, the people sought the bodies of the victims and were distressed because they could not find the head of Edmund. But it was found through the baying of an old grey wolf who seemed to be guarding it. Eventually the place where the martyred king was buried was adorned with offerings and became a shrine, much visited. Then a stately Abbey was founded to honour his memory and became a great place of pilgrimage, known as St. Edmunds Bury, famous throughout Europe.

BURY ST. EDMUNDS

King Canute

In 1016 Canute came to the throne of a much larger kingdom. He was, of course, the son of King Sweyn, the Danish ruler who had laid waste much of the English countryside during his conquests. Canute's empire extended from Bristol to the Arctic Circle, but he was a very different man from his father. Wise and tolerant, he sought many ways to placate his new subjects and made many generous offers to the Church in order to secure their willing co-operation in establishing firm but just rule throughout the land. In fact, it was Canute who laid the foundation of the future greatness of Edmunds Bury, which was to become Bury St. Edmunds.

The present-day town of Bury St. Edmunds really began to take shape in 1066, at the time of the Norman Conquest, for then the Abbot was a Frenchman named Baldwin who was able to prevent the destruction that took place in so many towns throughout the country. He immediately began planning and building. At the time of the Domesday Book survey of 1086, between 300 and 400 houses had been built and a square preserved for markets, this was the present Angel Hill. Five gates were established, churches were built in addition to the Abbey, and Bury had become an important centre by the beginning of the twelfth century.

Magna Carta

Although the Magna Carta was signed at Runnymede, its birthplace was here in Bury on the 20th of November 1214, when twenty-five of the most powerful Barons in England met in the Abbey Church and took an oath to force King John to accept it; hence 'Cradle of the Law'.

During the next 700 years Bury suffered setbacks and many difficulties but progressed to the point where, in 1914, the Bishop of St. Edmundsbury was enthroned in the Cathedral Church of St. James.

From the beginning, agriculture has been the life blood of Bury, when it prospered so did Bury, when the industry suffered so did Bury. Today the town still reflects the upward and downward trends of agriculture. The installation and growth of many light industries has helped to stabilise the economy.

Any attempt to see all that Bury St. Edmunds has to offer to the visitor in one day must of necessity fail. Few towns have so much that is both interesting, beautiful and of historic significance as Bury.

Angel Hill

The ancient town-planners of Bury did well to provide two open spaces, one for God and one for man. The former is now Angel Hill and the latter the Market Place. Any exploration should start from Angel Hill, where can be seen a veritable cavalcade of English building through the centuries. The ruins of the Abbey Church are in the grounds, which survive intact as a delightful garden park. The Cathedral of Edmundsbury was the church of St. James, and the church of St. Mary has a most impressive interior. The latter two are a little south of Angel Hill. The two impressive Abbey gateways, one Norman and one fourteenth century, give on to the Abbey Grounds, which run right down to the River Lark and the Abbot's Bridge of the thirteenth century.

Clock Museum

Still in Angel Hill, the white Athenaeum, with an Adam ballroom and a quite wonderful series of pictures of old Bury, should be seen. The Georgian style Borough Offices blend with the many dignified Georgian houses, of which Angel Corner is perhaps the finest; it also houses an outstanding collection of clocks and timepieces covering the centuries; it is said that Bury had a clock in the twelfth century. At one time clock-making was an important local industry and some fine timepieces came from Bury.

There are some lovely houses in Eastgate Street, notably the Fox Inn, at which many pilgrims stayed. Churchgate Street bisects the town from the Norman Tower on Angel Hill and is one of the medieval streets. On the left in Whiting Street is the 400-year-old Congregational Church and in Churchgate is an early eighteenth-century chapel. At the top of Churchgate Street on the right is the Guildhall of the fifteenth century, with thirteenth-century porch; in this old building the town council met from 1606 to 1966.

The Corn Exchange is a fine colonnaded building that was to be demolished in 1958; public reaction was so loud and instant that the decision was promptly reversed. Both the inside and outside are well worthy of examination. The Nutshell, said to be Britain's smallest inn, and Cupola House, of the early seventeenth century, are both delightful in different ways. Close to the Corn Exchange is a chemist's shop that, since 1781, has been a pharmacy. Nearby, on a well-restored building, is a statue of St. Edmund. The Tudor House has a fine corner-post carved to the likeness of Henry VIII. These are the most important of the older buildings of Bury.

Ickworth

Three miles south-west of Bury St. Edmunds is the National Trust property of Ickworth, which consists of 1,700 acres of parkland, some formal gardens with a quantity of cedars, evergreen oaks, redwoods, etc. The design of the house is as eccentric as its builder, the fourth Earl of Bristol, and dates from 1794. The central rotunda, which is 100 feet high, is flanked by two long, curving wings with an overall length of 700 feet; the public is admitted at certain times.

Packhorse Bridges

In the country immediately west of Bury St. Edmunds there are some lovely, unspoiled villages, among which Dalham is, perhaps, the best. Here, the fourteenth-century church with original wall paintings should be seen. At Moulton there are still two packhorse bridges.

Pakenham Windmill

The countryside north and east of Bury consists of large arable fields and patches of woodland. The A45 leads eastwards to Ipswich and, indeed, to Felixstowe. About halfway to the village of Woolpit, to the north of the A45, is Pakenham Windmill, which is still used to grind corn. Woolpit itself has a Decorated and Perpendicular church where there is possibly the finest hammerbeam roof in Suffolk.

Suffolk Fairies

Also in Woolpit are the brickyards where originated the expression 'The little green men of the Woolpit brickyard', to describe the Suffolk fairies. A short distance nearer Stowmarket, and in East Suffolk, is Haughley Park, an early seventeenth-century manor house with delightful gardens. It is open to the public on certain days. Gedding Hall, some six miles south of Woolpit, is another Tudor manor house, with a moat and parts of the drawbridge. Gedding Hall is a private residence.

Six miles from Haughley Park lies the agricultural town of Stowmarket.

STOWMARKET

Population: 8,750
Early Closing Day: Tuesday
Market Day: Thursday

ESSENTIALLY, STOWMARKET IS AN AGRICULTURAL MARKET town, although today there are a number of light industries. The known history of the town goes back to the Saxons but, since many Roman relics have been found in the immediate district, it may be inferred that they also had a settlement here. There are two Roman roads nearby, one, from Colchester to Caister, is largely followed by the A140 today; the other is more difficult to place, but can be followed from Cooks Green to Rattlesden. The Manor of Stowmarket was recorded in Domesday Book.

Old Buildings

Few really old buildings remain in Stowmarket, but the parish church and the vicarage are both worth a visit. The vicarage is sixteenth century, of half-timbered construction and, although alterations have taken place, a great deal of the original building remains. The church is largely from the Decorated period with some additions since. There are a number of interesting features and the vestry door is 500 years old. The Fox Hotel is another interesting house, of indeterminate age, but certainly a coaching inn. In the Butter Market is a business house that was an inn and is possibly from the fifteenth century. In the Market Place are a number of

Tithe Barn

A museum of great local interest is housed in a tithe barn at Abbot's Hall; this barn is itself of great interest for it was the tithe barn of the Abbot of St. Osyth and certainly dates from medieval times.

Six miles west of Stowmarket among the country lanes south of the A45 is the village of Rattlesden, with a delightful group of seventeenth-century houses around the Early English church. In this area there are many very lovely villages in a countryside that, as one journeys south, towards the Constable Country, begins to lose its strictly cultivated agricultural aspect and becomes far more naturally picturesque.

Needham Market

Needham Market, the only town between Stowmarket and Ipswich, is in the centre of the rich Gipping Valley and is growing fast. There are some attractive period houses and a church with a notable hammerbeam roof; the design is such that one wonders how it remains in position. A little to the west of the A45, just before entering Ipswich, the laneways will take the visitor to Nettlestead, where part of an Elizabethan mansion in red brick can be seen. Between here and Ipswich there is little of interest.

The southern part of West and East Suffolk, the 'Constable Country', is described in Section 9.

Ancient House, Ipswich

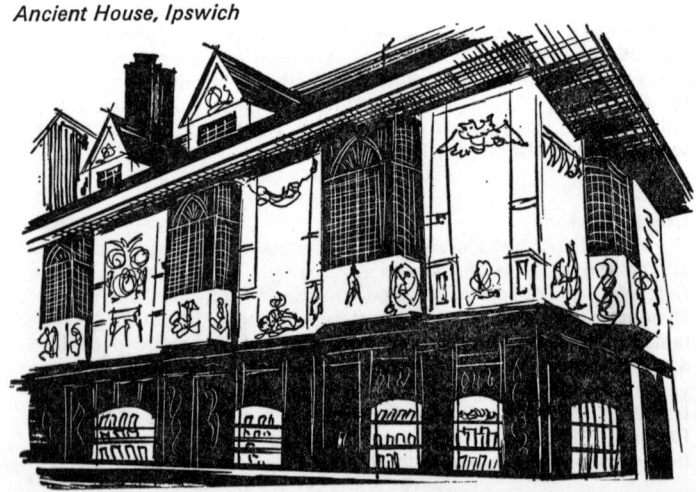

Section 8 North Essex Coast

HARWICH AND DOVERCOURT

Population: 15,300
Early Closing Day: Wednesday
Market Day: Friday
Tourist Information: (N) Caravan, Parkeston Quay 🛏
(summer only)

HARWICH AND DOVERCOURT, which together form one borough, are reached by passenger ferry from Felixstowe or by the A604 from Colchester. While Harwich is an important port, the headquarters of the Trinity House Authority (who are responsible for the lightships, buoys and all pilots around the coasts of Great Britain), Dovercourt is a residential area and a small and pleasant resort.

The Port

Like all busy ports Harwich is a great attraction to visitors. Boats and steamers of all kinds can be seen either in the Naval Base, at the Trinity House Quay, at Parkeston Quay (where the passenger steamers leave for many ports on the Continent), or at the old Navy-yard Wharf, where cargo steamers load for destinations all over the world.

Halfpenny Pier

There are a number of historic old houses in Harwich; note the Foresters in Church Street and the Three Cups Hotel, which is associated with both Drake and Nelson: it faces the Guildhall. Several streets have been restored by the council, notably West Street, King's Quay Street, King's Head Street and Church Street. Facing the Town Hall is the Halfpenny Pier, where the ferries leave for Felixstowe and Ipswich.

Treadmill Crane

Straight across the Stour, at Shotley, in Suffolk, is the Royal Naval Training Establishment H.M.S. *Ganges*. St. Nicholas Church, although rebuilt in 1825, has a twelfth-century font and some monuments from the medieval church. The church register contains a record of the marriage of Christopher Jones, the Master of the *Mayflower*, on its voyage to America in 1620. On Harwich Green is the Treadmill Crane, a relic of the early days of shipbuilding.

The Lighthouse

The Dovercourt Lighthouse is the last in a series, and of considerable interest. During the seventeenth century, coal shipments from Newcastle-upon-Tyne to London increased to such an extent that a great many lights were fixed at many points along the coast; two were built at Harwich in 1665; one was a crude coal-burning fire while the other was a primitive candlelit tower. These functioned until 1818, when they were replaced by brick towers but, owing to the continual building up of the sand on Landguard Point, these were again replaced by the Dovercourt Lights which finally became redundant; the channel into Harwich Harbour is now marked by buoys.

Holiday Attractions

At Dovercourt a walk along the Marine Parade brings into view the chief holiday attractions; boating lake and model yacht pond, tennis courts and bowling green, open-air swimming pool and putting green, the Cliff Pavilion and some extensive playing fields; these are a few of the amenities offered. Beacon Hill makes a fine breezy point from which to watch the passing ships.

Captain Fryatt

The parish church of All Saints was probably Norman, one blocked window remains of this period; the nave is late twelfth century while the staircase to the rood loft is still there. In the churchyard is the grave of Captain Fryatt of the S.S. *Brussels* who, with Nurse Cavell, was shot by the Germans at Bruges in 1916.

Riverside Walks

There are some nice riverside walks along the Stour west of Parkeston, while, for the naturalist and ornithologist, the coast south of Dovercourt offers endless opportunities—as it does for the yachtsman. Three to four miles south of Dovercourt there is an almost landlocked stretch of water enclosing Horsey Island, Hamford Water and The Wade, as well as a number of tiny islands. To the immediate north of this salting are the low, unspoiled cliffs of the Naze. All this piece of country offers some fine, if short, walks where the rush of city life can be completely forgotten.

The Naze

From Harwich and Dovercourt the A136 travels south through the village of Great Oakley, some four miles beyond which there is a turning to the east for Walton-on-the-Naze and Frinton, two quiet and delightful resorts. Frinton has an exceptionally fine sandy beach with some colourful gardens along the cliff-tops, for here the cliffs reappear to surprise one. West of the town there are tiny villages, backwaters and streams among the fields which are all untouched by

NORTH ESSEX COAST

industry. Walton-on-the-Naze is almost surrounded by water, for the saltings inland of the Naze very nearly reach the sea at the northern end of the town. Here again, clean sandy beaches, with a pier, a boating lake and other amusements along the sea front, make Walton an ideal family resort, while the low cliffs run from the town to the point of the Naze without anything to spoil the natural beauty. Six miles south of Frinton is Clacton-on-Sea.

CLACTON-ON-SEA, HOLLAND-ON-SEA, AND JAYWICK SANDS

Population: 37,950
Early Closing Day: Wednesday
Market Day: Tuesday
Tourist Information: (R) Town Hall, Station Road
(R) Marine Parade 🛏 (summer only)

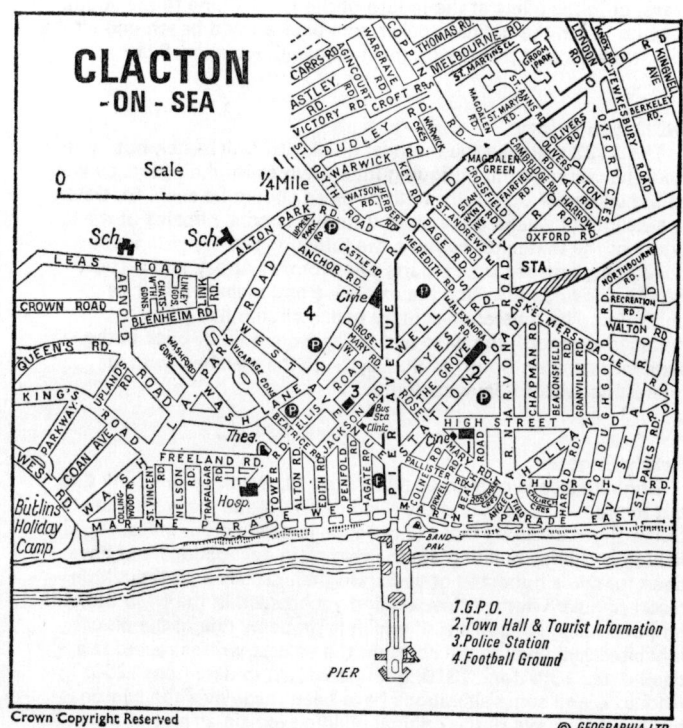

1. G.P.O.
2. Town Hall & Tourist Information
3. Police Station
4. Football Ground

Crown Copyright Reserved © GEOGRAPHIA LTD.

EAST ANGLIA

CLACTON-ON-SEA IS ONE OF THE foremost resorts on the east coast. It enjoys an enviable situation protected from the north winds. The beaches are extensive and safe and extend from Holland-on-Sea to Jaywick Sands, a distance of about four miles. Just about every possible entertainment and recreational facility is provided, the central point being the Pier, with pavilion, theatre, swimming pool and many other entertainments. There is a children's zoo, a Peter Pan railway and first-class playgrounds provided.

Beautiful Gardens

To many people the greatest joy of Clacton will be the gardens, which are extraordinarily beautiful and extend throughout the town. Among the other facilities are the day-trips to France, the Fishing Festival, a Carnival and many contests of various kinds. The countryside immediately around Clacton is among the loveliest in Essex; there are unspoiled villages, areas of marsh and endless river deltas where birdlife can be observed. There are also forested areas where the walker may enjoy life. North or south of Clacton the sailing enthusiast will find quiet waters among the islands behind the Naze, or in the inlets at the mouth of the River Colne to the south. It is, however, the holiday-maker who likes a good beach and all the fun of the seaside resort who most enjoys Clacton-on-Sea.

St. Osyth Priory

The A133 will take the motorist quickly to Colchester, but by that route he will miss the intriguing little town of Brightlingsea, as well as the village of St. Osyth; both of these should be seen. St. Osyth is a delightful village quite apart from the historic remains of the priory of the thirteenth century, the fifteenth-century gatehouse beautifully flint-decorated, parts of a Norman Abbey and a Tudor Palace, the ruins of which are extensive and include a fine art collection. The thirteenth-century parish church has a fine hammerbeam roof; the nave and aisles were built of brick in the sixteenth century. South of St. Osyth are the marshes, with an interesting walk to Jaywick Sands.

Brightlingsea

Brightlingsea is only three miles from St. Osyth as the crow flies, but the road passes round the head of one of the many little inlets of the River Colne so that the distance is nearly eight miles. Oyster-fishing and boat-building are the two main occupations and have been for some hundreds of years. Brightlingsea is a pleasant little resort popular with wildfowlers and yachtsmen. In the High Street is an hotel named Jacob's Hall which is probably one of the oldest inhabited buildings in the country; the earliest written record is a deed dated 13th June 1315, but it is known to date from 1250. Additions and some alterations have been made over the centuries but the main parts of the original building remain as part of the hotel.

Mersea Island

The estuary of the River Colne is west of Brightlingsea. Here, many inlets and pleasant waterways surround Mersea Island, where the large village of West Mersea is a mecca for yachtsmen and those who prefer a quiet and peaceful holiday. For many centuries West Mersea has been famous for its sail-making and boat-building as well as for the local oysters. The village is nine miles south of Colchester on the B1025. One road traverses the island from west to east and brings within easy reach the whole of the long sea-shore of occasional beaches and great mud-flats where the sea birds and waders feed undisturbed; for this is above all an island where nature still rules and absolute peace can be enjoyed.

Blackwater Estuary

It is not necessary to return to Colchester in order to follow the coast southwards to Maldon. There is a delightful road through the villages of Peldon, Great Wigborough, Tolleshunt D'Arcy and Goldhanger, while the village of Tollesbury is a little to the south and nearer the sea. This road skirts the marshland which forms the northern bank of the estuary of the Blackwater River and where Tollesbury forms a quite useful centre. Of the above villages, Tolleshunt D'Arcy is well worth a stop to see the unusual fifteenth-century church (unusual in being built of stone in a land where nearly all building is of flint) and the sixteenth-century Hall with a

St. Osyth Priory

brick-and-stone bridge dated 1585. At nearby Tolleshunt Major is Beckingham Hall, a half-timbered brick-built house of the sixteenth century in a large courtyard surrounded by a brick wall of the same period. Some panelling dated 1546 is now in the Victoria and Albert Museum. It is seven miles from Tolleshunt D'Arcy to Maldon at the head of the Blackwater estuary.

MALDON

Population: 15,000
Early Closing Day: Wednesday
Market Days: Thursday and Saturday

MALDON HAS OFTEN BEEN DESCRIBED as the 'Pearl of the Estuary Towns of Essex'. From the yachtsman's viewpoint it is certainly very high on the list of yachting centres, for it sits comfortably at the head of the wide clean sweep of the River Blackwater which is safe from the storms that beset the shorter and less sheltered estuaries.

For The Historian
The town itself is a very charming blend of old and new, a good shopping centre with all the modern amenities yet still retaining a great number of ancient churches, inns, shops and houses going back to the thirteenth century. For the historian or the lover of ancient architecture Maldon is one of the most rewarding towns in East Anglia.

For The Naturalist
Since the district abounds in marshes and unofficial bird sanctuaries Maldon is rightly popular with the naturalist and the ornithologist. The fisherman, also, will find much variety and excellent sport.

For the holiday-maker there is much to delight: the promenade along the river bank, the Marine Lake, the Boating Pool, parks and gardens with a glorious countryside and the Blackwater River and estuary to be explored.

Unique Library
Three towers, St. Peter's, the Moot Hall and All Saints tend to dominate the skyline and distinguish Maldon from many other towns. The tower of St. Peter's is fifteenth century, but undoubtedly replaced an older one, for the nave and chancel collapsed in 1665. Prior to 1244 there were two parishes, St. Peter's and All Saints. The brick building against the tower of St. Peter's, on the site of the nave, was erected in the late sixteen- or early seventeen-hundreds by Dr. Thomas Plume and contains some 6,000 books in eighteenth-century

Coggeshall   Paycocke's—detail of wood carving

Bury St. Edmunds   Norman Tower and South Front of Cathedral

Ely — Cathedral Tower and Ely Porta

Cambridge — Corpus Christi

NORTH ESSEX COAST

bookcases and the walls are lined with some fine Jacobean panelling. Many of the books are extremely rare, if not unique. It is open to the public at certain times.

All Saints

The church of All Saints stands in the highest part of High Street, the site of the most ancient part of the town. That part of the church facing the High Street is fourteenth century and the range of varied and traceried windows should be seen, the triangular tower should also be noted. The All Saints Vicarage was built early in the fifteenth century, certain additions have been made since, the timber frames have been exposed and a few minor alterations made but the greater part of this building is original.

Ancient Church

St. Mary's Church, which stands by the waterfront, is historically the oldest, for it was recorded in 1056. Structurally, the lower part of the tower is of fourteenth-century origin. St. Andrew's at Heybridge is an exceptionally interesting Norman church built in the twelfth century, alterations and some rebuilding took place in the fifteenth century.

Blue Boar

The Blue Boar Hotel is one of the oldest hotels in East Anglia. Although the frontage with the Georgian porch is eighteenth century a great deal of the building dates from the fourteenth, when Richard II was on the throne. The lounge and the dining-room date from about 1490. Across the yard is a portion of this fine old inn that dates, in its oldest parts, from the early thirteen-hundreds; this part was built before bricks came into general use and is therefore constructed of Essex oak and Essex clay. In its earliest days it was the residence of the De Veres, Earls of Oxford, and became an inn in 1573. Among the other notable inns of great age are the Swan and the King's Head.

Leper Hospital

Close to Maldon West station, now out of use, are the ruins of the Leper Hospital of 1164; for centuries St. Giles Hospital has been in use as a farm store but is now well cared for and can be seen by the public on request. Among the interesting features are the re-used Roman bricks. Just outside the town and not far from St. Giles Hospital are the very interesting remains of Beeleigh Abbey, which was founded in 1180. Much of the Abbey Church and some of the adjacent buildings were destroyed at the Dissolution of the Monasteries, but a great deal remains, including much from the thirteenth century. One wing of the Calefactory (monk's warming-room) is a lovely, mellowed, timber-framed Tudor structure with brick nogging. The public is admitted at certain times.

Moot Hall

In the High Street, a little west of St. Peter's Tower, is the Moot Hall, easily recognised by the overhanging clock. This fine old building was presented to the town in 1440 and is constructed almost entirely of bricks. It is still in use for various council purposes for it houses the Court Room, the Council Chamber, the Muniment Room and a stairway to the roof from which vantage point the town and many miles of the coast and surrounding countryside can be seen.

Link With U.S.A.

Among the many notable men connected with Maldon were Sir Edwin Landseer, the great animal painter, and Laurence Washington, the great-great-grandfather of George Washington, the first president of the United States.

Popular Harbour

Maldon's present-day claim to popularity must, in great part, be due to the very beautiful and very calm waters of the Blackwater estuary. Here, yachtsmen of little experience can with safety enjoy their sport, for there is plenty of room and, during the season, a host of boats of all classes. The more skilful can reach the open sea in twelve miles where, north or south, there are a number of ports and endless inlets and estuaries among the marshes of this fine yachtsman's and wildfowler's coast.

All Saints Vicarage, Maldon

Section 9 The Constable Country, Braintree and Colchester

THE NAME 'CONSTABLE COUNTRY' generally refers to that part of Suffolk and Essex in which the great painter was born, and where he lived and worked. For the sake of convenience in this guide it is being slightly extended to include a little more of Essex than, strictly speaking, it should.

The ancient market town of Sudbury is probably as good a point as any from which to explore what is held by many to be the most beautiful part of East Anglia; for on either side of the River Stour the countryside is completely different from the rest. From the mouth of the Stour as far as Bures the valley is well wooded with scores of tiny waterways, their winding little valleys joining the river. Short, steep little hills replace the gentle slopes farther north and nature has the appearance of having endowed Constable's land with unending growth and beauty.

SUDBURY

Population: 15,000
Early Closing Day: Wednesday
Market Days: Thursday and Saturday
Tourist Information: (L) Sudbury Library, Market Hill 🛏

SUDBURY IS AN EXCELLENT INTRODUCTION to the Valley of the Stour for it contains more than its share of the beauty of old and historic buildings. So does the valley itself, as well as all the little towns and villages from East Bergholt, Constable's birthplace, to Clare. As with the whole of south Suffolk and north Essex, Sudbury owes its past importance and its magnificent churches to the humble sheep. The sale of wool brought prosperity to these parts from the thirteenth to the early eighteenth century.

Modern Town

While today Sudbury is a modern town catering for a wide and prosperous farming district it has a great deal to show the visitor from its past. There are three historic old parish churches. St.

Gregory's is the Mother Church and dates from 1370; note the fifteenth-century choir-stalls, the font cover and the east window. St. Peter's is at the top of Market Hill in the centre of the town; some Norman work will be found in the tower, the rood canopy and the fifteenth-century Alderman's Pall, both extremely rare survivals, should be seen. All Saints has a good deal of fine fifteenth-century work, including the north and west doors of the tower and the pulpit.

Salters Hall

Among the many fine old houses the Chantry, with a magnificent carved corner post, and Salters Hall, with wood carving and the date 1450 over the door, take pride of place; both must be fourteenth or fifteenth century in origin with little if any alteration. In Cross Street the old Moot Hall is a fine example of the sixteenth-century house, while across the river the Bull Inn dates from about 1600. There are many excellent Georgian houses and some from an earlier date. Stour Street is generally considered the most picturesque.

Gainsborough

This is, of course, Gainsborough's town and reminders of him are everywhere; his statue is a fine one and the house where he was born in 1727 has been well renovated and is open to the public at certain times; it contains a representative collection of his paintings.

About seven miles to the east of Sudbury, in fine farming country, is the village of Boxford, where many half-timbered houses and the fourteenth-century church add to its natural charm; the fourteenth-century wooden north porch and the rare font-cover with doors should be seen.

HADLEIGH

Population: 5,000
Early Closing Day: Wednesday
Market Day: Monday

NEXT ALONG THE ROAD TO IPSWICH (the A1071) is the ancient centre of the wool and cloth trade, Hadleigh. Around the church of St. Mary there is a remarkable set of buildings; the fifteenth-century Guildhall is half-timbered and has two overhanging storeys. The Deanery Tower of 1495 is the only surviving remnant of the archbishop's Deanery. It is built of brick with embattled turrets six storeys high. Through the town there are many houses dating from the sixteenth and seventeenth centuries.

The church is one of the largest in Suffolk and dates from the thirteenth century. The chancel roof, the 600-year-old Angelus bell (one of very few left), are two features that should not be missed.

THE CONSTABLE COUNTRY

Stour Valley

To follow the River Stour from Sudbury to Dedham and East Bergholt is to make one of the loveliest motor runs in East Anglia; this can best be achieved by crossing to the south bank of the Stour at Sudbury by the Ballingdon bridge and then turning left along the river to Bures, where the river can be re-crossed and the northern bank followed through all the glorious villages and scenery that Constable knew and loved.

The village of Bures is a pleasant little place on the Suffolk–Essex border and boasts a church of the thirteenth to fifteenth centuries. This has a remarkable wooden effigy of a knight which was carved in the fourteenth century. A little farther down the river is Nayland, one of the gems of this part of East Anglia; it sits comfortably alongside the River Stour in one of its many glorious reaches and has quite a lot of fifteenth- and sixteenth-century houses to show; outstanding among these are the White House and the Queen's Head Inn. Alston Court in Church Street is impressive even among the remarkable half-timbered houses of the Constable Country; built in 1450 and added to in 1524 it has been little altered since. Those who are interested in buildings of this period will find in Alston Court one of the finest. Three miles north-east, Stoke-by-Nayland is another of the delightful villages with which this countryside abounds; the fine Perpendicular church should be seen. Between Stoke-by-Nayland and the very bonnie village of Higham is Thorington Hall, a National Trust property, which can be seen by appointment only.

At Stratford St. Mary there are two magnificent Tudor houses and the medieval tolbooth; the church is another wool church and very finely decorated. The village itself is delightful and was an important coaching stop.

Nayland

Dedham Vale

East Bergholt and Dedham should be taken in one visit, for in the former Constable was born and in the latter he went to school; the walk between the two places was the source of much inspiration and resulted in his painting of 'The Cornfield'. Many are the lovely old half-timbered houses in East Bergholt, some date from the time of Flemish weavers and a number are in virtually original condition. The church tower was never completed so that the bells have perforce to be housed in a bell-cage in the churchyard. Flatford Mill, which is a field study centre, and Willy Lott's Cottage, both subjects of inspiration to Constable, are much as they were in his time; both are National Trust properties and may be viewed from the outside. Both the mill and the cottage date from the seventeenth century and, combined with the immense natural beauties of the site, make a visit very rewarding although the site has been somewhat spoiled by modern amenities. There are several farms in the area over which the National Trust hold covenants; these can be seen by appointment.

Sir Alfred Munnings

Dedham is another very beautiful village, with many old houses and a church that entirely fits the prosperous wool merchants who built it; the short journey from Dedham to East Bergholt should be made on foot. There is a footpath through National Trust property by the river to Stratford St. Mary; about two miles in length it covers some of the most beautiful scenery in a very beautiful area. Castle House, Dedham, was the home of Sir Alfred Munnings and now houses an exhibition of his work; it is open two days a week. Among the many houses that should be seen are the Sun Hotel and the Marlborough Head Inn, both of the sixteenth century, and Constable's old Grammar School, dated 1732.

Between the River Stour and Ipswich there are many lovely villages and much fine, well-wooded country. Two places are of particular note. On the A1071 halfway between Ipswich and Hadleigh is Hintlesham Hall; a Tudor mansion, it is the scene of an annual July Arts Festival. Wenham Hall, which is a little west of the A12 some four miles from East Bergholt, is a unique house of the thirteenth century, and is among the oldest surviving examples of brickwork; it was a fortified Manor House but has the appearance of a fortress. Six miles north-east of Wenham is Ipswich, county town of Suffolk.

Delightful Clare

Constable's Country north of a line from Haverhill to Ipswich has several of the loveliest little towns in Suffolk, but not one large town. Haverhill, on the border with Cambridgeshire, is almost entirely industrial and, apart from being a good shopping centre, will be of little interest to the visitor.

A few miles west on the Long Melford road the small town of Clare is one of the most delightful of country towns, with little to upset the picture. Half-timbered houses, tiled houses, Georgian houses and a magnificent wool church delight the eye. In addition, Clare has the most complete remains of any Augustinian Friary in the country and a unique feature in Suffolk known as the Camp; this is an earthwork whose origin is lost in antiquity. Part of the keep of the Norman castle can be viewed. Among the wealth of lovely old houses dating from the late twelfth century are the following: The Ancient House, The Grove, Chapel Cottage or Wentford Chapel, the Bell Hotel, the Swan Inn, Cliftons, the Nethergate Hotel and Stour House; these are the finest in a remarkable collection.

Saxon Crucifixion

Nearer Haverhill, on the B1061 at the tiny village of Kedington, the church of St. Peter and St. Paul dates from the thirteenth century and among the many treasures the fifteenth-century screen and a carved Saxon Crucifixion are outstanding. Another very charming village is Stoke-by-Clare, which can be reached by country lanes from Kedington or by the main road from Clare; here a number of old cottages and the church give dignity to a very lovely village.

Cavendish

The village of Cavendish, which is nearly three miles east of Clare, is often described as the nicest village in England. Certainly the medieval church and a group of thatched cottages set in an extremely beautiful countryside make Cavendish at least one of the most beautiful villages.

Long Melford

Set in the picturesque valley of the Stour, as are Clare and Cavendish, is one of the gems among the small towns of Suffolk; Long Melford, whose history goes back to Roman days and which was one of the centres of the wool weaving industry, has preserved a great deal of its old buildings and nearly all its atmosphere of the past. The church in particular should be seen; it is rated one of the finest in a county of fine churches; the fifteenth-century stained glass (there are a hundred windows altogether) is probably as fine a collection as can be found anywhere in one church. On the very beautiful green stands the church, Melford Hall of 1550 and the Holy Trinity Hospital Almshouses of 1573. Melford Hall is open to the public and is the property of the National Trust. The village green is where the annual fair is held. In the old days this was celebrated as a horse-trading fair and the gypsies often gathered there, horse-coping being one of their skills. Readers of *Romany Rye* will recollect that George Borrow delivered a 'Long Melford' during his fight with the Flaming Tinman, that is, a punch which he learned at the prize fights which were part of the 'Fair'. The old Grammar School and the half-timbered Bull Inn with a galleried courtyard should also be seen.

Lavenham

Six miles north-east of Long Melford is the little town with an unrivalled reputation in East Anglia. Lavenham has a legacy of very lovely old buildings that must be unequalled in any town of similar size. The church of St. Peter and St. Paul dates from the fourteenth and fifteenth centuries, is a truly magnificent example of the wool churches and regarded, in some quarters, as one of the finest in England. The fourteenth-century rood-screen and fifteenth-century glass are among the best of many excellent features. Among the many delightful old houses there are a few which stand right out as examples of their period; the Wool Hall of 1500, a number of Tudor shops, the absolutely superb De Vere House, a number of houses in Church Street, the Grammar School, Shilling Old Hall, The Swan Hotel, The Guildhall of 1529, which is National Trust property, the Woolstaplers and many others of rare quality that portray the fine workmanship of the days when these wonderful old houses were built; and many of them were erected in the very early fourteen-hundreds.

Kersey Village

Situated among the country lanes about two miles north-west of Hadleigh is a village named Kersey that claims, with good reason, to be one of the most beautiful in England; the reasons are many, but chiefly because the one road crosses the valley and the tiny River Brett by ford. The fifteenth-century church stands on the hill while Priory Farm encompasses the remains of the thirteenth-century priory. Weavers' cottages, half-timbered houses, some thatched and some tiled and many colour washed, all blend superbly into a very beautiful picture.

West of Sudbury

The 'Constable Country' west of Sudbury lies in Essex, a county which is sometimes regarded as industrialised and not particularly attractive. This may be so as far as those parts near London are concerned, but central and northern Essex is as picturesque, as beautiful and little spoiled as any part of this country. There are many places made famous by such writers as Dickens, many famous old coaching inns and a wealth of half-timbered houses and cottages of the Tudor and Elizabethan periods.

Castle Hedingham

At Castle Hedingham, some seven miles south-west of Sudbury, the keep of the castle which was built in 1140 still stands and is regarded as one of the best examples of its kind in the country. The village, which is below the castle, has some good medieval and Georgian houses as well as a Norman church.

Farther north, near the Cambridgeshire border, Steeple Bumpstead, once a pleasant little village, has been swallowed by a tide of new housing. Six miles south-west by the country lanes brings the visitor to Great Sampford, where the church of St. Michael, which was rebuilt in the fourteenth century by the Hospitallers of St. John, still retains the south chapel from an earlier church.

Link with Brontës

In the immediate vicinity there are several other villages of interest and attraction. Finchingfield is a particularly nice village with some old houses and an attractive green with a pond, while Great Bardfield and Wethersfield have very interesting churches. Book-lovers will be interested to note the name of Patrick Branwell Brontë among the list of former curates of Wethersfield Church. The father of the famous Brontë family began his ministry here before going northwards to Thornton, near Bradford, where he married and where his remarkable children were born. Not far from Finchingfield is a post-mill with the miller's house quite close to the road.

Round Church

Although Halstead is still largely an agricultural small town, it is fast becoming industrialised. Less than three miles to the north on the A131 at the village of Little Maplestead is one of the five round churches in England; it was built in 1340 by the Knights Hospitallers of St. John and is of exceptional interest.

Gosfield Hall

Just west of the A1017 near Halstead stands a fine Tudor house with a gallery and 'secret room'. Though remodelled from time to time it is largely unspoiled and may be seen by the public on Wednesday and Thursday afternoons between 14.00 and 18.00 hours, May–September.

Post Mill

On the road from Halstead to Braintree a turn might be made to the village of Bocking Churchstreet, where the post-mill should be seen. Two or three miles farther and the visitor arrives in Braintree.

BRAINTREE

Population: 24,839
Early Closing Day: Thursday
Market Day: Wednesday

THE SITUATION OF BRAINTREE on the high ridge between the River Pant or Blackwater on the north side, and the River Brain on the south, has served it well; the Romans built their Stane Street along this ridge and established a camp at Braintree; in later centuries the pilgrims came this way to Bury St. Edmunds and Walsingham, so Braintree grew famous for its comfortable inns, many of which still exist although a lot have succumbed to the ravages of time or the requirements of modern building.

Since the fourteenth century Braintree has been engaged, as was most of the southern part of East Anglia, in weaving cloth; today, silk and man-made fibres form a great part of the textile industry. In addition it is the centre of an agricultural area and, although not primarily a holiday area, is, nevertheless, a good centre from which to explore the neighbourhood.

Four miles south of Braintree, near Silver End, is Cressing Temple; in 1135 this manor was given to the Knights of St. John and was their earliest English possession; in the early sixteenth century it became a farm and today still has two magnificent barns, one dated 1450 and the other 1530; some authorities date them much earlier.

Twelfth-century Glass

Witham, some seven miles south of Braintree, is changing quickly from a town with its roots in agriculture, and particularly in seed growing, to a large industrial complex planned for 25,000 people. A completed by-pass has improved the town centre tremendously and it is now a pleasant stop, but not a holiday centre. A little north-east of the town is the village of Rivenhall End where, in the midst of parkland, the church of St. Mary and All Saints is worth a visit to see the twelfth-century glass said to be some of the best in the country.

Near the village of Tiptree, now the centre of a fruit-growing district, Layer Marney will be found of interest; the mansion of Layer Marney, known as the Layer Marney Towers, was built as the gatehouse to a mansion that was never completed. It is the largest of its kind in the country and has some fine terra-cotta decorations. The church which is near the gatehouse was rebuilt in brick in the early sixteenth century.

Paycocke's

On the A120 six miles east of Braintree are two Coggeshalls, Great and Little; the former has the National Trust property of Paycocke's, which is a richly ornamented merchant's house of 1500; it possesses much finely carved woodwork. In addition, the Woolpack Inn of the late fifteenth century is certainly worth a stop. At the latter there are the remains of a Cistercian Abbey of 1140, the Abbey Gate Chapel of St. Nicholas remains and is in part an interesting example of the early use of bricks.

One of the most impressive, and one of very few, original Norman churches survives at the village of Copford Green, which is some four miles west of Colchester and a little south of the A12. The nave, chancel and apse are original, the wall paintings of the twelfth century were restored during the nineteen-hundreds.

COLCHESTER

Population: 86,000
Early Closing Day: Thursday
Market Day: Saturday
Tourist Information: (N) 4, Trinity Street 🛏

COLCHESTER, SITUATED ON THE RIVER COLNE only eight miles from the sea coast, owes its growth and much of its prosperity to this fortunate geographical location. Before the coming of the Romans there was a Celtic Settlement there and in the first century A.D. the British king in the south-east was Cunobelin, Shakespeare's 'radiant Cymbeline', who ruled that part of the south-east from his very prosperous capital of 'Camulodunum', which lay to the south of the river bank. He and his people appear to have had a thriving import and export trade with Europe to judge from the rich gold and silver articles and ornaments found in the burial-mound at Lexden Park. Indeed, the high quality of the grave-furnishings suggest that this

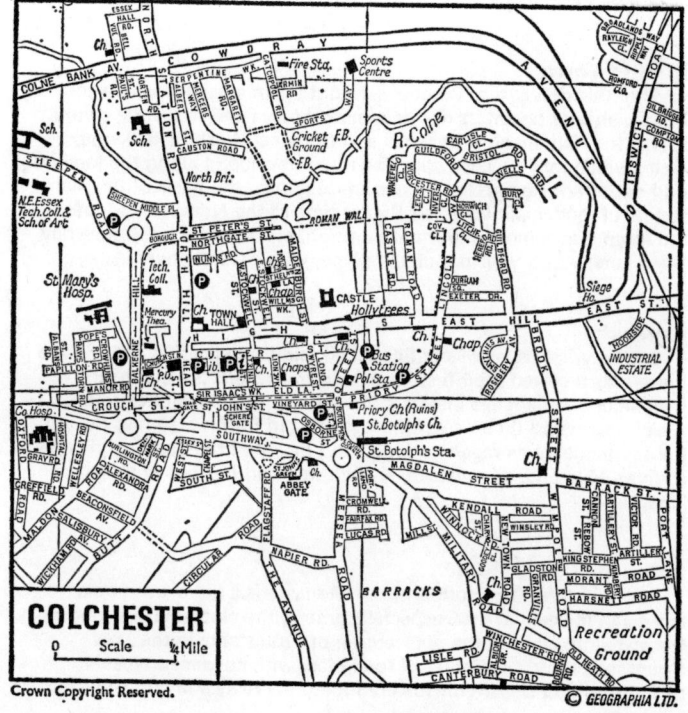

Boadicea

During the Roman invasions in the reign of the Emperor Claudius, A.D. 43, 'Camulodunum' fell and became thereafter a stronghold and haven of veteran Roman legionaries who formed a 'Colony' and taxed the indigenous people very heavily to support the tracts of land they took for themselves and for a Temple they built. In A.D. 60 Boadicea, Queen of the Iceni, summoned her people to war. She was the wife of King Prasutagus who had paid tribute to Rome in return for retaining rule over his part of the kingdom. At his death the Romans seized his realm, scourged the queen cruelly for daring to resist them and finally outraged her young daughters. The wronged queen and her warriors fell upon 'Camulodunum' at a time when the main Roman force was away on the Welsh border. The British destroyed the 'Colony' and its Temple and swept on victoriously through south Essex, to London. Though later defeated, her forces annihilated and herself driven to suicide, the story of this British queen has been remembered always—perhaps as an early example of 'resistance' to a reputedly invincible enemy!

Market Town

After this defeat the 'Colony' was not again established as such, but Colchester began its rise as a market town and industrial centre. It was fortified afresh with walls and the great West, or Balkerne, Gate, which may be seen still. The town developed along the familiar grid pattern of Roman towns and these remain the basis of the main streets of modern Colchester! By the time of the Norman Conquest the town was a most important borough, recorded by the Domesday Book survey as a well-populated place, with several churches.

Expansion

On the whole, Colchester flourished fairly steadily and in 1189 the burgesses received their first Charter from Richard the Lionheart. To its market and fisheries interests the town added the cloth trade, which prospered there, and although the old fortress fell into decay the town itself was much enlarged and included the outlying villages such as Mile End, Greenstead, Berechurch and Lexden as virtual 'suburbs'.

Refugees

Following the Dissolution of the Monasteries, there was some recession in trade at first, especially among the cloth-makers, but by the sixteenth century the persecution of Protestants in the Low Countries brought an influx of foreigners with advanced weaving techniques and skills. This fostered the great revival in cloth-making.

COLCHESTER

With this revival other local trades prospered too and Colchester was much improved by the building of many solid burgher mansions and handsome houses.

Royalist Seizure

The Civil War brought new destruction to much of the town, for though most of the merchants and people were Parliamentarians, Colchester was successfully seized by Royalist forces and held for the king for eleven weeks. General Fairfax, the famous Parliamentarian General, appears to have dealt harshly with the townsmen despite the fact that, by and large, they had not been particularly willing supporters of the Royalist cause. As well as putting two of the Royalists before a firing squad, he fined the starving townsmen heavily and obliged them to dismantle their defences.

Napoleonic Threat

It was during the Napoleonic Wars that Colchester again became a garrison town, but after Waterloo the military presence declined and for a time so did trade. But there was still opportunity for fresh market development and, of course, the fisheries. For a time it seemed uncertain whether Colchester could effectively operate commercially, but the coming of the railways in 1843 and the further establishment of a new garrison stimulated commerce once more. This time the military presence was made permanent and the railways led to the establishment of a vigorous engineering industry so that, whatever the fluctuations of political or economic affairs, the town had certain staples upon which to rely. After each World War, expansion consolidated the importance of Colchester into the thriving municipality and river port which it is today.

Museums

There are three museums, which show most of the smaller items of Colchester's history and development. The Castle Museum houses the oldest material, i.e. pre-Roman through to medieval times; 'Holly Trees' displays the later exhibits; and All Saints' Natural History Museum has a most interesting exhibition dealing with the natural history of Essex generally, and the ecology of the country around Colchester in particular. There is an aquarium, and various living and some mounted exhibits, also a diorama of the salt-marshes at Fingringhoe Nature Reserve.

Roman Castle

The Roman Walls which once encircled the 'Colony' are still largely in being and can be seen. Inside the ancient 'walled town' is Castle Park and the Castle itself—now only the Keep of a once mighty fortress which took up ground from the High Street to the north wall. The Keep contains much that is of tremendous interest and it was built upon the site of the ancient Temple of the Romans. Portions of other buildings were uncovered here in 1950.

Abbey Gateway

Close to St. Botolph's Street and the bus park is St. Botolph's Priory, which was founded in 1100. Although only the west front and a portion of the nave survive they are extremely impressive. The gateway of St. John's Abbey is another ecclesiastical monument which keeps alive Colchester's rich past. It was built in the fifteenth century and is decorated superbly with flintwork panels in the traditional East Anglian style. It is also all that remains of the Abbey, founded originally in 1096. Both are in the hands of the Dept. of Environment and are open to the public.

Holy Trinity Church

Among the many lovely churches in Colchester, Holy Trinity is the oldest and most architecturally interesting. The tower dates from A.D. 1000 and is the only Saxon building in the town. One Saxon doorway is complete and the west wall of the nave is older even than Saxon. There are few buildings of such antiquity in this country. St. James's is the largest of the old parish churches and some parts of it date from the twelfth century. During the Middle Ages additions were made in the grand style of the wool churches, and some of the flintwork is notable as there are not many such examples of this kind of, specifically East Anglian, decorative work extant in Colchester.

Dutch Quarter

The area between the Castle grounds to the east and Stockwell to the west is called the 'Dutch Quarter' because of its many fifteenth-century gabled houses, though indeed some of them are older and were there long before the influx of Flemish weavers to whom the appellation 'Dutch' was usually applied. Maidenburgh Street, leading to the 'Quarter', also has some picturesque half-timbered and plastered cottages, and more quaintly still, is paved at the top of the road with granite blocks with a track for cart-wheels.

Queen Street was for many centuries the venue of the St. Denis Fair which signalised the opening of the oyster-fishing which was so important to the town, for 'Colchester natives' are not easily rivalled.

Siege House

In East Street stands the 'Old Siege House', carefully restored early in this century. During the famous Siege of 1648 in the Civil War its timbers were peppered with bullets which came, oddly enough, not from Fairfax's artillery outside but from Royalist positions on the right bank of the river. This lovely old half-timbered, handsomely gabled building was the property of the owners of East Mills and it was they who had it so well restored and preserved.

COLCHESTER

Bourne Mill

Beyond the gates of the Infantry Barracks the road leads down to the stream which provided water power for Cannock Mill and Bourne Mill. This latter mill is the property of the National Trust and may be visited by request. The most interesting feature of the building is its gables, which have curved steps crowned with pinnacles. The mellow stone of the Elizabethan decoration is charming.

Roman Walls

Time should be spared by the visitor for a walk around the Roman Walls of ancient Colchester. Starting from St. Mary's Steps in Church Street the tour may be accomplished in less than an hour and will certainly give an excellent idea of the historic cradle of the present flourishing town.

The Town Hall

The present home of Colchester's civic dignity, the Town Hall was built as the result of a competition for design among architects. The competition was won by a man named John Belcher and, although his interior plans aimed more at space and grandeur than practical use of space, the outside is very handsome and its tower dominates the High Street and the skyline of Colchester in a very dignified style. The most important room in the Town Hall is called the 'Moot Hall', after the old Saxon name for such civic buildings. In October this room is the scene of the famous 'Oyster Feast', which is a very good time to be in Colchester.

Holly Trees, Colchester

Section 10   Cambridge and the Isle of Ely

CAMBRIDGE

Population: 104,000
Early Closing Days: Monday/Thursday
Market Days: Monday and Saturday
Tourist Information: (N) Wheeler Street

ALTHOUGH THE CITY OF CAMBRIDGE became especially famous in the Middle Ages through the fame of its great seats of learning in the University, it was in fact already well known in history. It was an established trading centre by reason of its position at the navigation head of the River Cam and had been also a defensive fort for the Romans, Danes and Normans. William the Conqueror commanded the building of a castle, on what is now Castle Mound, in an effort to check the successes of Hereward the Wake and his band of loyal Englishmen who held out so long in East Anglia.

Architectural Heritage

Cambridge today is the great social, commercial and cultural centre of the county, famous for the beauty of its buildings and for their lovely setting along the banks of the Cam. It is essential to allow time for a leisurely stroll through Cambridge in order to take in properly the magnificent architectural heritage of the colleges, chapels, galleries and museums, amid their lovely lawns and gardens. Thus one may absorb and appreciate fully the air of classic calm, the aura of the long tradition of learning and the overwhelming sense of history emanating from the very stones around one.

The Backs

Such a tour should start with the Cam itself, south of Magdalene Bridge, and the colleges to be seen from the riverside lawns known as 'The Backs'. Perhaps only Christchurch Meadow in Oxford can rival 'The Backs' for the juxtaposition of simple rural charm and elegant architecture. Cambridge has been called the 'University of the Poets', for many great ones have been enrolled among the students at the various colleges. Kit Marlowe was a Cambridge man, and so

CAMBRIDGE

were Robert Herrick and Andrew Marvell. John Milton, fair, dreamy and already inclined to Puritanism, was known as 'The Lady of Christ's'. On the other hand, John Cleveland, a minor poet and very much a king's man during the Civil War, was anti-Puritan and somewhat of a roistering temperament. Thomas Gray was at Peterhouse, the very oldest of the colleges, Wordsworth was at St. John's, and Coleridge was at Jesus.

Samuel Pepys

Other famous figures, besides poets, shed lustre on the colleges. Perhaps one of the most colourful and endearing of personalities was Sam Pepys, whose Diaries afford us such an intimate glimpse of life in a moderately prosperous seventeenth-century household. Pepys was also to become memorable as having worked to make the British Navy into a formidable force on the high seas and these efforts, too, are recorded in his Diaries, in the form of shorthand known as 'Shelton's' and only successfully transcribed in the early nineteenth century.

Some Other Writers

Lord Macaulay, the historian, was a familiar figure in Cambridge and in modern times names like those of the Powys Brothers occur in the rolls of Corpus Christi. J. B. Priestley, the Yorkshire-born writer, was a Cambridge man and so, for a time, was 'Louis Marlow' (Louis Wilkinson), writer and lecturer. Among distinguished women writers, Rose Macaulay and Virginia Woolf were associated with Cambridge.

The Colleges

King's, Clare, Emmanuel and Peterhouse are among the finest of the collegiate buildings, but, of course, everyone has an individual opinion on the subject. But there is at least one topic upon which all agree and it is that the chapel of King's is of quite outstanding beauty, with its intricate workmanship and fan vaulted roof of unsurpassed magnificence. The other undisputed glory of King's is the view of the College from 'The Backs'. The great windows in the chapel are the most complete and also the largest series of ancient windows in the world.

Visits

The Great Court of Trinity College must be seen; it is the largest University Court in the world and was built in 1610. Most of the Cambridge Colleges were founded in the fifteenth, sixteenth and seventeenth centuries, a few were earlier. It should be remembered that, unless a notice forbids entry, all the grounds and forecourts, as well as many of the ground floors, of the colleges are open to the public during the day, a few are open in the afternoon only.

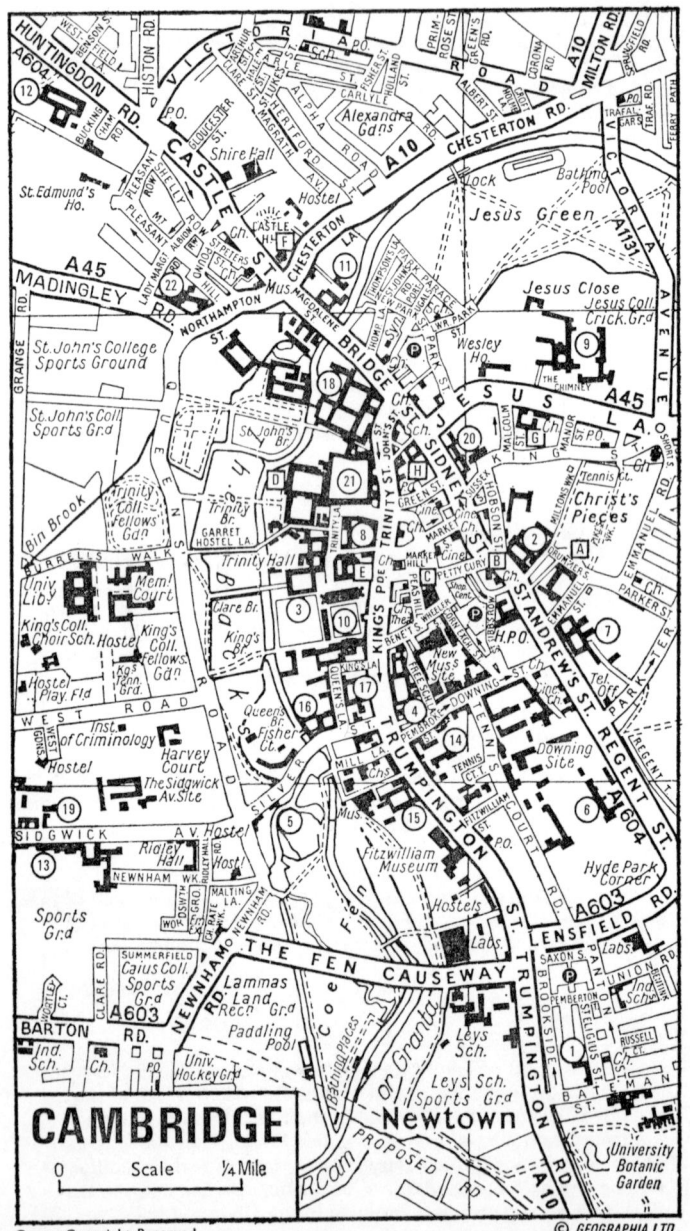

KEY TO PLAN OF CAMBRIDGE

Colleges

1. Cheshunt
2. Christ's
3. Clare
4. Corpus Christi
5. Darwin
6. Downing
7. Emmanuel
8. Gonville and Caius
9. Jesus
10. King's
11. Magdalene
12. New Hall
13. Newnham
14. Pembroke
15. Peterhouse
16. Queen's
17. St. Catharine's
18. St. John's
19. Selwyn
20. Sidney Sussex
21. Trinity
22. Westminster

Other Buildings

A. Bus Station
B. Civic Centre
C. Guildhall
D. Nevile's Court
E. Old Schools
F. St. Giles Church
G. Westcott House
H. Whewell's Court

Churches

Among the many very beautiful churches, most of which have treasures and architectural glories, is Great St. Mary's, in King's Parade, which was rebuilt in 1478. The Round Church (there are only five in England) follows the design of the church of The Holy Sepulchre in Jerusalem. The church of St. Benet's is notable for its tower, the oldest building in Cambridge. The upper window is an example of Saxon architecture and very rare.

Museums

Among the many museums there are two of exceptional interest. The Fitzwilliam, near Peterhouse, houses a large number of statuary, tapestry, archaeological discoveries and original manuscripts. The Scott Polar Research Institute in Lensfield Road will be of interest to many in this age of scientific research. Other museums are: Archaeology and Ethnology, Downing Street, Classical Archaeology, Little St. Mary's Lane, Folk, in Castle Street, Sedgwick Museum of Geology, Downing Street, Whipple Museum of the History of Science, Free School Lane, and Zoology in Downing Street.

Old Houses

A great deal of the charm of Cambridge derives from the narrow streets and passages, with many houses of note. Little St. Mary's Lane and Botolph Lane are two good examples. The Little Rose Inn in Trumpington Street is dated 1600 and is probably the oldest inn in Cambridge. Barnwell Abbey House, of 1678, is a half-timbered and brick building that was famous for quite a large number of ghosts. The small, thirteenth-century remains of the Cellarers Chequer House of the Barnwell Priory founded in 1092 is well worth a visit. The Eagle Inn in Benet Street is the last of the coaching inns.

The Environs

Just to the south-west, neighbouring Cambridge, lies Grantchester, ever-memorable for the poem by its most distinguished resident, Rupert Brooke, on 'The Old Vicarage, Grantchester', perhaps one of the world's most-quoted sets of verse. Its opening lines set the mood of wistful homesickness (the poet was writing in Germany):

> 'Just now the lilac is in bloom
> All before my little room
> And in my flower-beds, I think,
> Smile the carnation and the pink.'

The famous closing lines

> 'Oh yet, stands the church clock at ten to three
> And is there honey still for tea?'

must be the best-known lines Brooke wrote, aside from 'If I should die', and though today the church clock is not, in fact, fixed at 'ten to three', the village itself is so pretty as to make clear his unconquerable nostalgia.

The American Cemetery

Some three miles west from Cambridge along the A45, a secondary road branches off to the right for Madingley village. The A45 continues ahead, up a slight hill with, at the top, a post mill on the right. Shortly after, also on the right, is the entrance to the American Cemetery.

Senate House, Cambridge

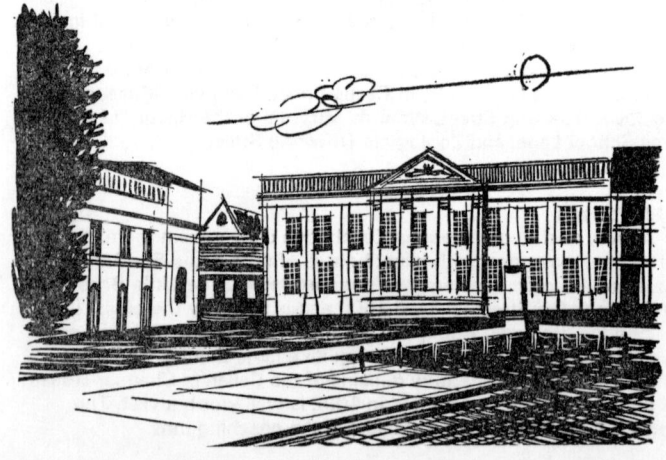

MADINGLEY

This is the great memorial to and burial place of those United States Servicemen who died whilst serving in Britain. Behind a screen of trees a long wall shelters lily-ponds and rose gardens. On this wall are inscribed the names of those who made the ultimate sacrifice that others might live in freedom and the dedication above the columns of names emphasises this point. Beyond the garden the white crosses stretch 'row on row' (as Colonel McRae the Canadian poet wrote in the First World War), and the only dead not represented are those whose bodies were returned to their homeland.

The Map Room and Chapel contains a truly spectacular wall chart of the world upon which are laid out representations of Allied ships and aircraft and their operation areas during the Second World War.

Set into the glass doors overlooking the hillside are reproductions of the escutcheons of the various States of the American Union, and above the great entrance doors are reproductions of the service badges of all the units concerned. At the eastern end of the Map Room is the Chapel. The cemetery may also be entered from the Madingley road and ample parking space is available.

Madingley with its Elizabethan Hall has many associations with historic events and royal personages. Charles I once hid there, and both Edward VII and George VI resided there when entered at the University. Today the handsome mansion, set amid noble cedar trees, is part of the University. The church of St. Mary Magdelene is mainly thirteenth and fourteenth century in construction. There are notable communion rails, beautiful sixteenth-century stained glass pieces and memorials to the Cotton family.

Earthworks

South-east lie the Gog-Magog Hills with notable earthworks; they are relics of the Iron Age, later refortified by the Romans. It is a fact that there is no land higher than these hills looking directly eastwards until the Ural Mountains are reached, bordering Siberia. Close by the Gog-Magogs is the Roman road, Via Devana.

Farther south lies the village of Sawston, with its sixteenth-century Manor House, home of the Huddlestone family. It contains notable family portraits, many lovely tapestries, much handsome panelling and is celebrated for its 'Priest's Hiding Place'.

Returning to the outskirts of Cambridge on the Trumpington road one passes the charming fourteenth-century church of SS. Mary and Michael, where may be found the second oldest brass in any English church.

Scattered around the University city are several of the charming villages known to and mentioned by Brooke in his Grantchester poem, among them, Cherry Hinton, Coton, Babraham, Ditton and others.

Six miles to the north-east of the city is the National Trust property of Anglesey Abbey. The thirteenth-century crypt below the house indicates that a monastic building belonging to the Augustinians was the original property, but in 1600 it was made into a house. There are glorious gardens belonging to the estate which was bequeathed to the Trust under the will of the first Baron Fairhaven in 1966.

NEWMARKET

Population: 13,200
Early Closing Day: Wednesday
Market Days: Tuesday and Saturday

HORSES! THE ONE WORD DESCRIBES and adequately conjures up this very pleasant town, which is given over almost 100 per cent to the 'Sport of Kings'. Indeed, several kings have been responsible for the fact. The hunt-loving King James I started it, when he built a hunting lodge there after his first visit in 1605, and the Stuart monarchs generally loved horse-racing, and horse-breeding. Indeed, Charles II, with his many mistresses and high-born but illegitimate children, was nick-named 'Old Rowley' by his loving subjects, after a famous stallion of that name belonging to the royal stables.

Sport of Kings

The splendid open heathland surrounding Newmarket has proved, of course, the ideal training and racing ground. William of Orange imported Arab-bred horses to improve the royal Stud and, among the Hanoverians, the Duke of Cumberland took an interest, and, until he had his quarrel with the Jockey Club, 'Prinny', the Regent, later George IV, was a frequent visitor to the Newmarket races. His brother the Duke of York was a keen race-goer and often stayed at the old Palace, which was finally sold, and then demolished, during the reign of Queen Victoria. However, royal interest in Newmarket revived under the influence of her lively son the Prince of Wales, afterwards Edward VII. This second 'Merry Monarch' (the original being Charles II) bequeathed a love of horses and racing to his descendants, all of whom are to be seen, upon occasion, following the aptly named 'Sport of Kings'.

National Stud

Not surprisingly, Newmarket is the home of the National Stud, one of the most modern in existence anywhere, and although at the present time there are a few other light industries in the neighbourhood, racing and horses remain the major interest and source of employment.

By-passed to the west, the town, on the London-Norwich road, is joined on its western side by several very pretty roads. These lovely beech-lined approaches to the town are among the most attractive avenues by which to enter Newmarket, and the open land north-east of these roads is one of the favourite places for exercise gallops. In fact, it should be remembered that across all the main arteries of this town one is likely to be held up while a string of horses crosses the road to the practice gallops. However, there are few sights more arresting than the spectacle of so many thoroughbred, delicately boned 'noble animals' in a string, lifting their heads at the prospect of stretching their legs across open country.

NEWMARKET

High Street

Newmarket High Street is an agreeable amalgam of pleasant Georgian and solidly Victorian establishments, together with some fairly harmonious modern additions. At the top of the High Street is an excellent vantage point from which to take stock of the place. The west side of the street has some of the town's most charming houses and away beyond the main road is Warren Hill, crowned with a plantation of trees set in a great circle.

The fountain erected in 1910 to the memory of Sir Daniel Cooper is at the south-western end of the High Street, while the north-eastern end is where the Fordham and Bury roads lead into the town by the old Green with its Victorian Clock Tower. The Congregational Church on the corner of Sun Lane and High Street stands on the site of the old royal residence, and the road behind it is called 'Palace Street'; it boasts a house said to have been occupied by Nell Gwyn. That enterprising young woman generally contrived to have a household adjoining anywhere that Charles II was staying, so there is every reason to believe she was often there.

Two buildings worthy of special note are the Rutland Arms Hotel, with a red-brick front, extensive stables and courtyard, and the Jockey Club, Georgian in origin, but now boasting a front designed in 1933 by Sir Albert Richardson.

The church of St. Mary, fourteenth–fifteenth century originally, is now mainly nineteenth century Restoration style. It is notable, however, for a medieval piscina which was uncovered during the restoration work. Tattersall's Sale Paddocks lie between the High Street and the Station Approach and, of course, many places and streets names recall names associated with the sporting fraternity and the royal patrons of the past. Rowley Drive, Queensberry Road, and Regent Court are a few examples.

Kirtling Tower

For those interested, it is worth making a diversion for some five miles to the south-east of Newmarket to see Kirtling Tower. It is a three-storey, half-moated gatehouse—all that is left of a once splendid mansion which was the property of the North family.

A little farther along the road from Burwell their are two Swaffhams. The first, Swaffham Prior, has a tower windmill, some delightful thatched cottages and a Henry VIII half-timbered house; then comes Swaffham Bulbeck, with a moated farmhouse, Burgh Hall, of 1650. Then come four houses of note: the Lordship House, clunch-built; the Merchants' House, dated 1711, which is a brick house with a Dutch gable; the Maltings, opposite and of 1697; lastly, the Abbey House of 1778, which incorporates the vault of the Monastery established in 1190.

Seven miles north-west of Newmarket on the B1085 is the National Trust property comprising the Wicken and Burwell Fens, a nature reserve of 730 acres; it contains some very rare examples of insect and plant life in a type of fen that is fast disappearing. Nearby is one of the now rare windmills. The village of Isleham is seven miles north-east of Newmarket and within the village is the Isleham Priory Church of 1100. The village church of the fourteenth century has a very fine hammerbeam roof and other attractive features.

Approaching Ely by the side roads east of the A142 the village of Chippenham will be passed; this is a squire's model village of attractive houses and cottages dating from 1800. Ely is eight miles from Chippenham on the A142.

ELY

Population: 10,750
Early Closing Day: Tuesday
Market Day: Thursday
Tourist Information: (L) 24, St. Mary's Street

WHEN ST. ETHELDREDA chose the lonely hilltop amid the fens and marshes as the site for a new religious house, the Isle of Ely was a wild and lonely area made up of tiny hamlets and scattered settlements. The Abbey, which this king's daughter and former queen of Northumbria founded, was to house both monks and nuns. In succeeding years, during which St. Etheldreda died, her place as Abbess was taken first by one of her sisters and later by her niece. In A.D. 870 the Abbey was pillaged and burnt by the marauding Danes and it was a hundred years later before St. Ethelwold was commissioned by King Edgar to reconsecrate and build a new abbey for monks of the Benedictine order.

King Canute

This was to become famed throughout the land as a place of music and scholarship and below the Abbey walls there grew up the houses of people who looked to the community for their guidance and employment. Here it was that King Canute came with his queen Emma and presented the Abbey with rich cloths and jewels for the shrine of its founder saint, and here he heard the beautiful choral chanting which inspired him to write his English ballad,

> 'Merrily sang the monks of Ely
> When Canute the King rowed by.
> "Row near the land, Knights," said the King,
> "And let us hear the monks sing." '

The Wake

It was among these wild fens and reed-clad marshes that Hereward the Wake, the last defiant English leader, resisted the Conqueror, refusing all offers of amnesty from the formidable Norman. Aided by the monks of Ely, outlawed but still surrounded by loyalist English, he waged a war of attrition against the Conqueror's troops. It was probably only through treachery that the Normans found the way through the fens to his stronghold and, in summer A.D. 1071, broke at last this heroic five-year resistance movement!

Henry I, the youngest son of William I, became king on the death of his unmarried brother William Rufus. He created Ely a bishopric, and after some vicissitudes in ensuing years the Abbey prospered at last and by the thirteenth century spent a great deal of money on beautifying and improving the great Cathedral. Two earlier places of worship preceded the Cathedral. The first was built in A.D. 673 and the second in A.D. 970, during the reign of Dunstan as Archbishop of Canterbury.

It was during the adornment of the Cathedral in the fourteenth century that the old choir and apse disappeared to make way for the magnificent Early English Presbytery. Then came the work of the 'flower of craftsmen', Alan de Walsingham, Sacrist of the Priory. Traditionally, as well as caring for and preserving the fabric of the Cathedral, he is credited with the design of the Lantern and Octagon and of the lovely Lady Chapel. He is said to have been a skilled goldsmith as well as a designer.

Iconoclasts

The Lady Chapel was of large dimensions and was built as an additional adjoining chapel reached through the north transept. It was said to have blazed with the glory of its medieval stained-glass windows, but these were destroyed by iconoclastic zealots during and after the Reformation period. Though the carving is much defaced, enough of the arcades remain to indicate how handsome it must once have been.

Walpole Gate

To the north of Palace Green is the Chantry, with some seventeenth-century exterior work and some eighteenth-century interior decoration. The great south gatehouse of the priory is known as 'Ely Porta', or Walpole Gate, and was once the boundary of the monastic precincts, dividing the calm cloistered world of the monks from the bustling city outside. Within the courtyard the Monks Granary, a fifteenth-century building, still stands. Probably there would have been the Abbey mill nearby. East of the Granary is the mound which was the site of the Norman 'motte-and-bailey'-type castle built during the wars between King Stephen and Queen Matilda. It served as a stronghold until the time of Edward I.

Still in the precincts of the Cathedral there is the long barn, now used as a gymnasium for the King's School; the Black Hostelry, Walsingham House, of 1335, and the almonry, with a vaulted undercroft, should all be seen.

Cromwell House

Outside the Cathedral precincts Cromwell House, now the Vicarage, St. John's Farmhouse, of the sixteenth century with a thirteenth-century monastic barn, the White Hart Inn, which is partly fifteenth century, and a number of small cottages on Waterside, which is the most picturesque street, should all be seen. There are a few more notable houses: number 22 Fore Hill and some Georgian houses in St. Mary's Street. On the south side of High Street the Steeple Gate can hardly be missed; it was built in the sixteenth century. The Quay, once known as the Broad Hithe and the river port for Ely, is now a centre and mooring for pleasure boats; it is little changed over the centuries.

Stretham Old Engine

At Stretham, on the A10 south of Ely, is the only steam beam pumping engine still in working order. It was built in 1831 during the course of work on the great fen-draining scheme. Above the engine-house is a museum displaying articles recovered from the drained fens.

CHATTERIS

Population: 5,490
Early Closing Day: Wednesday
Market Day: Friday

CHATTERIS IS A VERY NICE LITTLE TOWN with a friendly welcome for the visitor. It is as old as any place in the Fens, for it is situated on one of the tiny islands that dotted this country long before it was drained and roads constructed. The parish church dates from the thirteenth century, but was rebuilt a hundred years later after a fire. There is a most interesting museum with local exhibits from as far back as the Stone Age. There is some noted coarse fishing in the district and pike of twenty or more pounds are often caught.

MARCH

Population: 14,250
Early Closing Day: Tuesday
Market Days: Wednesday and Saturday

MARCH WAS KNOWN TO THE ROMANS, and the general opinion among experts is that it was already a thriving community when the Legions arrived in Britain. But it was definitely a much more developed community during Saxon times and, as the name implies, was established on the 'boundary', or 'march', which separated the 'East Angles' from the 'Middle Angles'. St. Wendreda, to whom March's exceptionally attractive church is dedicated, was a Saxon lady of very ordinary origins, though she proved to have been a most exceptional person who left her mark upon the religious life of her times.

By the Middle Ages, however, March had developed into a township with several guilds, and this indicates that it had become already a busy, and even important, place. One such guild was that of St. Wendreda, a very good account of which may be found in the town's Record Offices.

St. Wendreda's

This is a handsome edifice, built largely in the Perpendicular style, though the tower dates from the fourteenth century. Undoubtedly its crowning glory is the magnificent double hammerbeam roof above the nave. It represents the almost miraculous skill of the medieval wood-carvers. The roof displays 120 carved angel figures, most of which are projected from the hammerbeams, with their wings outspread almost creating the illusion of a great upward rush of flight, so much so that the truly imaginative might almost hear the air disturbance!

There was, of course, a church here in Saxon times. The steeple was built in 1400 and rises to 140 feet. One unusual feature worth noting is the passageway under the tower, which may preserve an ancient right-of-way. Among the large number of angels is a carving of the devil; it is difficult to spot but it can be found. Note also the two rather ferocious gargoyles which guard the entrance to the south porch.

WISBECH

Population: 17,560
Early Closing Day: Wednesday
Market Days: Thursday and Saturday

AS A FENLAND TOWN Wisbech occupies an exceptional position. It is an excellent place from which to tour northern and western Norfolk; it is rich in fine architecture of the past and has far more features of this type than any other Fenland town. It is a port and has been since the Romans carried out the first improvements to the mouth of the River Nene; today it has no railway links but instead is a first-class road centre.

From the holiday-maker's viewpoint it will be found one of the nicest towns imaginable. Rich in beautiful gardens, a first-class shopping centre with a very good market, Wisbech can offer the visitor most of the pleasant things of life.

The Brinks

The most notable features in the town are the two Brinks, one on either bank of the Nene; they are reputed to be among the most perfect Georgian streets in England. Peckover House, on the North

Brink, is a National Trust property and was built about 1722; it contains furnishings of about the same period and the garden contains some rare trees and plants. Numbers 14 and 19, on either side of Peckover House, are also National Trust properties but are open to Trust members by written appointment only.

In the years prior to the Norman Conquest it appears Wisbech was situated on the northern bank of the Nene; today, although on both sides of the river, the town centre is built around the site of the castle, the church, and the tree-shaded crescent which surrounds the site of the castle, with many Regency houses. Here also is the Wisbech and Fenland Museum, a place of absorbing interest.

The parish church of St. Peter and St. Paul is a notable and somewhat unusual church of Norman origin. The most unusual feature is the double nave. The very handsome tower, of the early sixteenth century, is detached and in the north porch of the tower will be seen a beautifully decorated fourteenth-century doorway.

Among the many other houses of note the Rose and Crown Hotel, with Tudor brick barrel-vaults and a most elegant eighteenth-century staircase, should be seen. Do a little quiet exploring, there is a lot to be found in Wisbech.

Thirteen and a half miles to the north-east is King's Lynn, where this journey around East Anglia commenced.

Windmill, Wicken Fen

INDEX

A

Acle	Page 40
Aldeburgh	72
American Cemetery, The	116
Ampton	85
Anglesey Abbey	117
Attleborough	57
Aylsham	49

B

Baconsthorpe Castle	49
Bacton	32, 33
Badingham	82
Bale	51
Banham Zoo	58
Barnby	83
Barningham Town	48
Barsham	84
Bawdsey	74
Beccles	39, 83
Bedingfield	84
Beeleigh Abbey	97
Belcher, John	111
Berney Arms Mill	39
Bigod Family	81
Billingford	61
Binham Priory	51
Bishops' Bridge	44
Blakeney	28
Blakeney Point	29
Blickling Hall	49
Blogg, Henry	32
Blundeston Church	40
Blythburgh	82
Boadicea	108
Bocking Churchstreet	105
Bonner, Bishop	54
Borrow, George	103
Boulge	81
Bourne Mill	111
Boxford	100
Braintree	105
Brancaster	26
Brandon	85
Breckland	7, 16, 23, 24, 63
Bredfield	81
Bressingham	59
Brightlingsea	94
Brisley	53
Broads, The	6, 10, 38, 40
Bromholm Priory	33
Brontë, The Rev. Patrick Branwell	105
Brooke	62
Brooke, Rupert	116
Brown, Capability	82
Browne, Sir Thomas	44
Bullfer Grove	51
Bungay	39, 61
Bures	101
Burgh Castle	67
Burnham Deepdale	27
Burnham Market	27
Burnham Norton	27
Burnham Overy	27
Burnham Thorpe	27
Burnham Westgate	27
Burwell Fen	120
Bury St. Edmunds	85
Butley	80
Buxton	46

C

Caister-on-Sea	32, 35, 37
Caley Mill	25
Cambridge	Page 112–115
Camulodunum	108
Cannock Mill	111
Canute, King	40, 87, 120
Castle Acre	63
Castle Hedingham	104
Castle Rising	24
Cavell, Nurse Edith	43
Cavendish	103
Cawston	50
Charles I, King	117
Charles II, King	59, 77, 118
Chatteris	122
Chippenham	120
Civil War	109, 110
Clabourne, William	23
Clacton-on-Sea	93–5
Clare	102
Cleveland, John	113
Cley-next-the-Sea	29
Colchester	107–111
Coleridge, Samuel Taylor	113
Coltishall	46
Constable, John	78, 101
Constable Country	7, 99–102
Copford Green	106
Cotman, John Sell	44
Covehithe	69
Crabbe, George	72
Creake Abbey	52
Cressing Temple	106
Cromer	31–33
Cromer Ridge	15
Cunobelin	107

D

Dalham	88
Dedham	102
Dedham Vale	102
Dennington	82
Dersingham	25
Dickens, Charles	77
Dilham	48
Diss	59–60
Ditchingham	62
Dovercourt	91–3
Downham Market	64–5
Duelling Stone	50
Dunwich	70

E

Earlham	45
Earsham	61
East Anglia University	45
East Barsham	52
East Bergholt	102
East Dereham	54–5
Easton Farm Park	81
Edward the Confessor, King	120
Edward III, King	75
Edward VI, King	54
Edward VII, King	117, 118
Ellingham	62
Ely	120–2
Euston	66
Euston Church	85
Eye	84

F

Fairfax, General	109
Fakenham	52, 53
Felbrigg Hall	48
Felixstowe	74

INDEX

Fens, The	Page 8, 16
Finchingfield	105
Fisher's Theatre	47
Fitzgerald, Edward	81
Flatford Mill	102
Flemings Hall	84
Fordham	64–5
Framlingham	81
Framlingham Castle	81
Frinton-on-Sea	92
Fritton Lake	40
Fryatt, Captain	92

G

Gainsborough, Thomas	78, 100
Garrett, Elizabeth	73
George IV, King	118
George VI, King	117
Gog Magog Hills	116
Gorleston-on-Sea	35, 36
Gosfield Hall	105
Granchester	116
Gray, Thomas	114
Great Bardfield	105
Great Coggeshall	106
Great Hautbois	46
Great Livermore	85
Great Sampford	105
Great Yarmouth	32, 34–7
Grimes, Peter	73
Grimes Graves	65
Guestwick	50
Gwyn, Nell	119

H

Hadleigh	100
Halstead	105
Hanseatic League	22
Happisburgh	33
Harleston	60
Harwich	91–3
Haughley Park	89
Haverhill	102
Heacham	25
Hedenham	62
Henry I, King	121
Henry II, King	74, 76
Henry III, King	19
Henry VII, King	69
Henry VIII, King	54, 88
Hereward the Wake	16, 112, 121
Herrick, Robert	113
Herringfleet	40
Heveningham Hall	82
Hevingham	49
Hingham	55
Hintlesham Hall	102
Holkham Hall	27
Holland-on-Sea	93
Holly Trees	109
Holt	31
Horsey Mere	33
Horsham St. Faith	49
Houghton Hall	62
Houghton St. Giles	52
Hoveton	39, 46
Hunstanton	25, 26

I

Icklingham	85
Ickworth Park	88
Ingham	85
Ipswich	76
Isleham	Page 120
Ixworth Abbey	84

J

James I, King	118
Jaywick Sands	93
Jockey Club	118, 119
John, King	19, 87

K

Kedington	103
Kenninghall	58
Kersey	104
Kessingland	69
Ketteringham Manor	57
Kilverstone Wildlife Park	66
King's Lynn	19, 23
King's Lynn Festival	22
Kirtling Tower	119
Kyson Hill	80

L

Lakenheath	85
Lamas Manor	46
Landguard Point	75
Landseer, Sir Edwin	98
Lavenham	104
Layer Marney	106
Leiston	71
Lessingham	33
Lexden Park	108
Lincoln, Abraham	44, 53, 55
Lincoln Seal	33
Little Barningham	48
Little Coggeshall	106
Little Maplestead	105
Little Walsingham	51, 52
Long Melford	103
Lott's Cottage, Willy	102
Lower Ufford	80
Lowestoft	67
Lowestoft and E. Suffolk Marine Society	68

M

Macaulay, Lord	113
Macaulay, Rose	113
Maddermarket Theatre	44
Madingley	116, 117
Magna Carta	87
Maldon	96
March	122–3
Marlowe, Christopher	113
Marsham	49
Marvell, Andrew	113
Mary Tudor, Queen	54, 58
Maylon Bridge	46
Melford Hall	103
Mersea Island	95
Mettingham Castle	84
Mildenhall	85
Milton, John	113
Minsmere	10
Minsmere Bird Sanctuary	71
Moulton	88
Mundesley	32
Munnings, Sir Alfred	102

N

Narborough	64
National Stud	118

INDEX

National Trust .. Page 22, 26, 27, 29, 33, 35, 49, 50, 51, 53, 57, 62, 64, 71, 80, 84, 88, 101, 102, 103, 104, 106, 111, 117, 119, 124	
Nayland	101
Naze, The	92
Needham	60
Needham Market	90
Nelson, Lord	27, 36, 47, 64
Nettlestead	90
New Buckenham	58
Newmarket	118–19
Newton by Castleacre	64
Norfolk Wildlife Park	50
North Barningham	48
North Barninghall Hall	48
North Cove	83
North Creake	53
North Elmham	52
North Walsham	32, 46–7
Norwich	41–5
Norwich Castle	24, 44

O

Old Buckenham	58
Old Rowley	118
Old Siege House	110
Orford	73–4
Ostend Holiday Village	33
Otter Trust	61
Oulton	39
Oulton Broad	68
Overstrand	32
Overy Staithe	27
Oxburgh Hall	64
Oyster Feast (Colchester)	111

P

Paine, Tom	66
Pakenham Windmill	89
Pakesfield	68
Paston Family	47, 48
Paycocke's	106
Peasants' Revolt	47
Peddars Way	64
Pepys, Samuel	114
Plume, Dr. Thomas	97
Potter Heigham	40
Powys Brothers	113
Priestley, J. B.	113

R

Railway Museum (Sheringham)	31
Ranworth	40
Rattlesden	90
Raynham Hall	53
Reedham	39
Reepham	50
Rendlesham Forest	79
Richard the Lionheart	80, 108
Richardson, Sir Albert	119
Ricklinghall Inferior	84
Rivenhall End	106
Rolfe, John	23
Royal Norfolk and Suffolk Yacht Club	68

S

St. Benet's Abbey	40
St. Olave's Priory	40
St. Osyth	94
Salle Church	50
Salthouse	29
Salthouse Broad	Page 29
Sandringham	24
Sawston	116
Saxlingham Nethergate	60
Saxmundham	81
Saxted Green	82
Sco Ruston	46
Scolt Head	26, 27
Sea Palling	33
Seckford, Thomas	80
Sewell, Anna	36
Shelton	60
Sheringham	30–1
Shipdham	55
Shotley	91
Sidestrand	32
Sitomagus	71
Sizewell	71
Slaughden	72
Smith, Captain John	23
Snetterton	58
Snettisham	25
Somerleyton Hall	40
South Creake	52
South Raynham	53
South Wooton	23
Southwold	14, 69–70
Southwold Jack	70
Stalham	38, 46
Staverton Forest	80
Steam Engines	59
Steeple Bumpstead	104
Stiffkey	28
Stoke-by-Clare	103
Stoke-by-Nayland	101
Stowmarket	89
Stratford St. Mary	101
Stretham Old Engine	122
Sudbury	99–100
Suffolk Wildlife Country Park	68
Sutton Hoo Treasure	81
Swaffham	63–4
Swaffham Bulbeck	119
Swaffham Prior	119
Swanton Morley	153

T

Tattersall's Sale Paddocks	119
Terrington St. Clements	23
Thetford	65–6
Thetford Heath	88
Thorington Hall	101
Thorpeness	71
Thursford	52
Timworth	85
Titchwell	26
Tollesshunt d'Arcy	95
Tolleshunt Major	95
Townsend, "Turnip"	28
Trunch	48
Tunstall Forest	74

U

Ufford	80

V

Vancouver, Captain George	22

W

Walberswick	70
Walcott	33
Walton-on-the-Naze	92
Warham	51

INDEX

Warren Lodge	Page 65
Wash, The	19
Washington, George	98
Wattisfield	84
Watton	54
Waxham	33
Weeting Castle	65
Wells-next-the-Sea	28
West Acre	64
West Mersea	95
Wethersfield	105
Weybourne	29, 31
Wicken Fen	120
Wickham Market	81
Wilkinson, Louis	113
William of Orange	118
Willy Lott's Cottage]	102
Wisbech	Page 14, 123-4
Witham	106
Wiveton	29
Wolferton Station	24
Wolsey, Cardinal	78
Woodbridge	79
Woodbridge School	80
Woolf, Virginia	113
Woolpit	89
Wordsworth, William	113
Worstead	46
Wroxham	39
Wymondham	56-8

Y

Yoxford	82

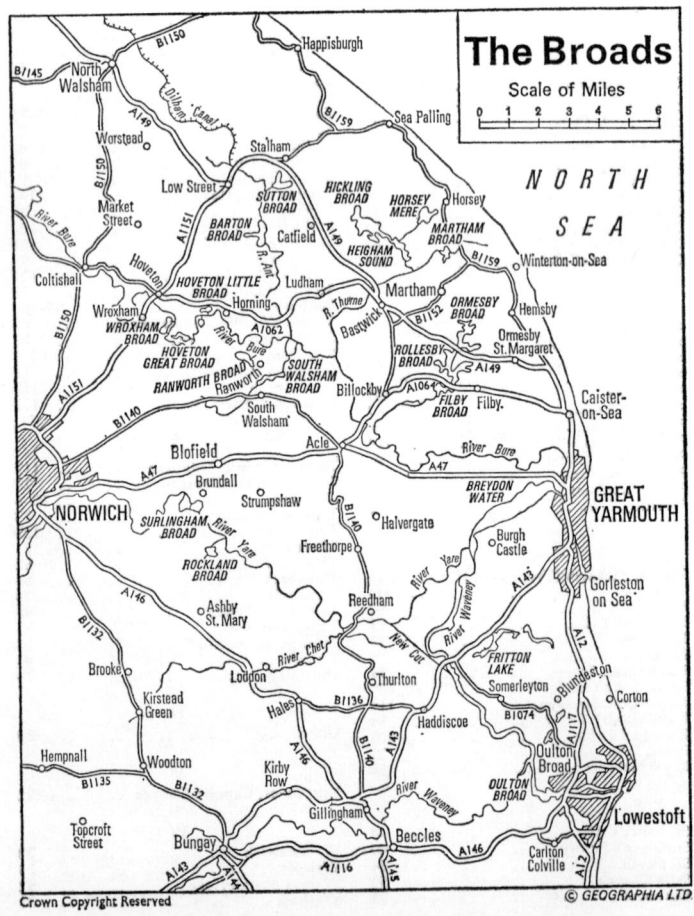

Crown Copyright Reserved © GEOGRAPHIA LTD.